Everyone Belongs to God

# Everyone Belongs to God

Discovering the Hidden Christ

## Christoph Friedrich Blumhardt

*Compiled and edited by Charles E. Moore*

PLOUGH PUBLISHING HOUSE

Published by Plough Publishing House
Walden, New York
Robertsbridge, England
Elsmore, Australia
www.plough.com

19  18  17  16  15      1  2  3  4  5  6  7  8  9  10

Front Cover Image: *X-ray Manhattan* © Eric Drooker

Sources translated by Alan Stevenson, Miriam Mathis, and Jörg Barth

A catalog record for this book is available from the British Library.
Library of Congress Cataloging-in-Publication Data

Blumhardt, Christoph, 1842-1919.
  Everyone belongs to God : discovering the hidden Christ / Christoph Friedrich
Blumhardt ; compiled and edited by Charles E. Moore ; with a foreword by Jona-
than Wilson-Hartgrove.
    pages cm
  Includes bibliographical references.
  ISBN 978-0-87486-646-9 (pbk.)
  1. Kingdom of God. 2. Christianity and culture. 3. Missions. I. Moore, Charles
E., 1956- editor. II. Title.
BT94.B6175 2015
231.7'2--dc23

                          2014045173

Printed in the USA

Here, there is no Gentile or Jew,
circumcised or uncircumcised,
barbarian, Scythian, slave or free,
but Christ is all, and is in all.
*Colossians 3:11*

# Contents

# Foreword

## Your Gospel Is Too Small

**In every age,** God's people need prophets to help us see beyond our blind spots – to expand our vision of what God is about.

Jeremiah was a prophet. To a people in exile, caught between the false hope that their God would destroy Babylon and the despair of thinking God had forgotten them, Jeremiah proclaimed a new vision. The old images of God's faithfulness would no longer suffice. Yes, their God had saved humanity in an ark and washed away the wicked in a great flood. Yes, their God had brought them out of Egypt, drowning Pharoah's army in the Red Sea.

But a salvation that requires someone else's destruction is too small a salvation, Jeremiah proclaimed. To a people in exile, he wrote, "Seek the peace and prosperity of the city to which I have carried you into exile. Pray to the Lord for it, because if it prospers, you too will prosper" (Jer.29:7).

You will not be saved apart from your neighbors, the prophet says. Everyone belongs to God. Or, to quote another of the biblical prophets:

> It is too light a thing that you should be my servant
> to raise up the tribes of Jacob
> and to restore the survivors of Israel;
> I will give you as a light to the nations,
> that my salvation may reach to the end of the earth.
>
> *Isaiah 49:6, NRSV*

Jesus came preaching peace to all people. But he got into the most trouble for showing the religious insiders how the people they counted out often understood the advent of God's reign better than they did. Take Luke 4. For his first sermon in his own hometown, Jesus took a text from Isaiah, the prophet. And when he said that the great day of Jubilee had arrived for God's people, everyone rejoiced.

But when he pointed out that a Syrian soldier and a Gentile woman had more faith than anyone else in their day, the hometown crowd tried to throw him off a cliff.

Your gospel is too small, Jesus said. But no one wants the prophet to speak so directly to them.

Better to celebrate that the scripture is fulfilled in our hearing than to grapple with the ways God's Word forces us to expand our imagination.

But expand we must. At least, that's what the prophets tell us.

The text of the book you now hold in your hands is over a century old, but it contains the words of a prophet who was ahead of his time. At the beginning of the so-called "Christian Century," when science and progress seemed to be bringing Christendom to its full height of glory, Christoph Blumhardt heard a word that cut through his cultural formation and easy assumptions: Everyone belongs to God.

Cultural captivity is, of course, a far cry from exile, but the long march of Christendom, as we now see more clearly, took God's people as far from the Promised Land as Nebuchadnezzar's forces ever did. As in the Babylonian captivity, we face a dual temptation.

On the one hand, there are those who say, "All you've got to do is believe." God is greater than the forces of secularism and materialism, atheism and individualism. Yes, Western Christianity is compromised. But the pure in heart – those who *really* believe – can be saved right here, *right now.* All you have to do is bow your head and say this simple prayer. . . .

On the other hand, the cynics point out, the Good Book became the Bad Book in so much of the Western missionary enterprise. We over-evangelized the world too lightly, exporting cultural hegemony along with the faith, doing more harm than good. Christendom has failed, they say, and so it is best to leave the name of Christ behind. Do good, for goodness' sake. At the very least, try to do no harm.

In the midst of this crisis, I hear Blumhardt's words for twenty-first-century Christians in the same vein as Jeremiah's to seventh-century-BC Israel: "The Risen One wants to draw people to himself, and so propaganda for a particular confession of faith or church is no concern of his. You must stand up and represent the gospel of the kingdom that shines for all people, no matter who they are."

We cannot give up on the missionary enterprise because we have misunderstood and abused it. Instead, Blumhardt insists, we must reclaim the heart of Christian mission.

Our gospel has been too small. It is, indeed, too small a thing to think that the hope of the world rests in our ability to recruit others into a religion which has too often made us morally worse.

To confess that the hope of the world is Jesus Christ is to open ourselves to a kingdom beyond our control – beyond our imagination, even. It is to embrace the revolutionary notion that everyone belongs to God.

Though Bonhoeffer had not yet introduced the term when Blumhardt wrote these letters, it was in the midst of his own confrontation with the crisis of Western Christianity that he wrote of "religionless Christianity." Bonhoeffer had so little time to explore what this term meant, even less how one might practice it in the world.

But this volume fills some of that void. For it, we can all be grateful. Take and read the words of a prophet for our time.

*Jonathan Wilson-Hartgrove*

# Introduction

**Christoph Friedrich Blumhardt** (1842–1919), a
Lutheran pastor in Germany, was not at home either
in church or secular circles; his views seemed to challenge and disconcert everyone. And yet he possessed
a strange, infectious confidence in God's history and
an uncanny ability to see what it takes to bring the
gospel of Jesus Christ to the world.

Son of the renowned Johann Christoph Blumhardt,
a pastor in Möttlingen and later in Bad Boll, Christoph Blumhardt continued his father's work. But he
found himself increasingly alienated from the established German church and eventually broke with all
the outward forms of church life, clerical robe and all.
His exit from the institutional church was partly due
to his growing concern over the dire social conditions

around him, which eventually led him to take to the streets in support of the labor movement.

Though he served in the Wurttemberg parliament as a Social Democrat from 1900 to 1906, he could never really bring himself to be a tried-and-true party member. He returned to Bad Boll and in his later years sought to point those who would listen to him to a vision of God's kingdom that would bring about lively communities of faith where people could give themselves completely to God's future.

Richard Wilhelm was one of many who were greatly influenced by Blumhardt's fiery conviction that the advancement of God's kingdom – its here-and-now actualization – must take precedence over all else. When Wilhelm set out to become a missionary in China, he was already closely involved with Blumhardt. During his short service as an assistant pastor in Bad Boll, Wilhelm had been deeply moved and gripped by this spirit-filled man of faith. He went on to marry Blumhardt's daughter Salome. So it was of special significance to Blumhardt that Wilhelm and his wife went oversees to serve the cause of Christ. To him they were, above all, envoys of God's kingdom – a cause far greater than what was expected of missionaries.

In May 1899 the General Evangelical-Protestant
Missionary Society (Far East) assigned Wilhelm the
territory of Kiaochow, on China's Yellow Sea. Under
European duress, China had been forced to cede
this area to Germany on a ninety-nine-year lease.
As a missionary pastor in Tsingtao (fast becoming
a flourishing colonial city), Wilhelm was assigned
a threefold task: to be a pastor, spread Christianity among the Chinese, and promote understanding
between China and Germany.

Under Blumhardt's influence, however, Wilhelm
viewed the Missionary Society, of which he was
formally a part, as merely an outward instrument
serving the higher purpose of God's kingdom. He was
neither interested in traditional mission nor in representing Germany. He wanted something entirely new.

Blumhardt, for his part, felt a special responsibility
for the work of his son-in-law, whom he had so obvi-
ously influenced. This motivated Blumhardt to write
over a hundred letters to Wilhelm between 1898 and
1914.[1] Many of the selections that follow are extracts,
thematically arranged, from these letters. The rest
are from various sermons and lectures. (To help the

---

1   These letters are contained in their entirety in the forthcoming book, *Christ
in the World: Letters to Richard Wilhelm in China (1898–1914)*.

text flow, thoughts from various letters and talks have in places been synthesized, and transitional phrases added. Bible references have also been added for those wishing to explore the biblical foundation of Blumhardt's thought.)

Full of hearty warmth, Blumhardt's words radiate a fatherly care, even as they voice a prophetic battle cry for authentic Christian witness. The thread that runs through these selections is Blumhardt's unwavering belief in the living Christ as Lord over all. As Blumhardt saw it, Jesus claims the whole world for his own, not just the Christian world. No one is separated from Christ's love – neither the "unchurched" nor the "pagan," and especially not the oppressed. On the contrary, the will and purpose of the common person who thirsts for meaning and strives for justice, and the insights and longings of non-Christian peoples, originate in the will of God himself.

What then was Wilhelm's task as a missionary, and the Christian's broader task in the world as Christ's witness? It was to carry into the world, particularly the non-Christian world, "the gospel of Jesus Christ, not the gospel of the Christians."

In the following pages the reader will discover more precisely the difference between these two gospels. Suffice it to say that the "gospel of the Christians" has little or nothing to do with the revolutionary message of Christ itself. Jesus did not come to found churches, defined by doctrine or ritual, but to set in motion a movement of the Spirit that would encompass nations and lead to inner freedom, peace, and social justice. For Blumhardt, the "gospel of Jesus Christ" has nothing to do with Christianity, Buddhism, or any other religion. "No longer religion against religion, but justice against sin, life against death."

The reader will see that Blumhardt was quite critical of various missionary efforts precisely because they concerned themselves with spreading Christianity on a Western pattern, instead of representing the reality of God's reign. Blumhardt's understanding of Christian witness flew in the face of the concept of mission held by typical mission societies. It still flies in the face of so many missionary and evangelistic efforts today. For Blumhardt, new ways to demonstrate God's love must always be sought; the thoughts printed here are a direct expression of that search for fresh paths.

Influenced by Blumhardt's down-to-earth message, Richard Wilhelm focused his efforts on improving the standard of living of those he worked with. This included establishing schools and hospitals, quite daring and novel at the time. Conflicts with the Missionary Society were inevitable. Unlike his peers, Wilhelm was simply not interested in propagating the Christian religion among pagans. Like Blumhardt, he viewed the noble manifestations of other religions without prejudice, even with reverence for God's work.

Admittedly, this sounds like the perfect recipe for syncretism or religious relativism, with Jesus' truth reduced to just one of many manifestations of truth. It is clear from these selections, however, that Blumhardt emphasizes the gospel of the kingdom – the revelation of God – as the supreme truth that fulfills humankind's deepest religious longings.

Blumhardt's thoughts and concerns are amazingly prescient. Long before terms like indigenization and contextualization became vogue, Blumhardt grasped that God's living Word always incarnates itself in earthly ways. In this sense, Blumhardt was a pioneer of a new kind of mission. And so his words speak directly to our time, where we see so much Christian missionizing yet so little of God's transforming power.

As in Blumhardt's time, our world is in the throes of much ferment, and in the West in particular there is increasing cynicism and skepticism towards anything Christian. Elsewhere in the world, Christianity, with its many sects and denominations, is flourishing and, according to some, having a healthy liberalizing effect. But for Blumhardt, and for an increasing number of Christians today, such a phenomenon is not necessarily a good thing. Under the guise of religion, the gospel has not only become adulterated, but God's power to effect a radical change here on earth has been stifled.

The question today for those who seek to represent the gospel more authentically is: How do we bring the gospel of Christ to a world that is in the grip of capitalistic materialism, increasingly secular, and resentful of religious façades that perpetuate injustice, without spreading a Christianity that is little more than a pie-in-the-sky religion among a world of religions? How do we demonstrate the good news of Christ's victory over suffering and sin and demonic powers in this world where masses of people are imprisoned in urban wastelands of poverty and despair? How can followers of Christ genuinely proclaim the new creation he promised when words, especially religious verbiage, have become cheap and when our lives and churches have so little to show?

Though his words may at times lack precision, Blumhardt clearly writes from a passionately moved heart. Theologically, there may be points with which one could take issue. Even his central assertions possess a remarkable duality, especially regarding the institutional church and the people of Christ, Christians and non-Christians, testimony by word and testimony by deed. Indeed, the wisdom he offers may at first appear "foolish" to those who demand theological exactitude.

A patient, generous reading of Blumhardt, however, should clear up any apparent contradictions. For instance, Blumhardt's critical comments regarding baptism and the attempt to make people Christians do not preclude the practice of baptism nor the need for conversion. Similarly, Blumhardt affirms God's working within history and culture, yet he is clear that civilization – with its technical, intellectual, and political development – is doomed without the truth that God revealed in Christ.

Blumhardt never claimed to be a scholar; he was a pastor at heart. Readers who long to faithfully stand their ground in the stream of the world as witnesses to God's coming kingdom will find no manufactured truths or artificial musings. For Blumhardt, making known the gospel was a matter of daring something in faith, of experimenting, and of finding new, concrete ways for God's kingdom to advance. His concern was that the message of Christ be brought to nations and peoples in a true, life-giving way, opening instead of closing doors to all those for whom Jesus died.

Blumhardt boldly believed that the earth and all its peoples belonged ultimately to God. He possessed an unwavering confidence in the advancement of God's new creation, even if it was "beneath the surface, in quiet, hidden ways." He held that in the midst of the storm and stress of world history, there have always been clearly recognizable signs of this clandestine advance. In an increasingly pluralistic world, the insights contained in this book can help us see the signs that are visible today – provided we are willing to have our conventional ideas challenged and our horizons broadened.

*Charles E. Moore*

**1**

# Keep the Kingdom in View

**In the kingdom of God** one cannot turn back. Therefore, strive for God's kingdom with every drop of
your blood (Matt. 6:33–34). The work you or I do is
incidental; we are only vessels of the Spirit that awaits
the future of God. Think about it: the kingdom of
God is in your midst – among a faithful people – and
it alone will be the starting point from which the
Savior leads his cause to victory. In all your work you
must hold firmly to the thought that the kingdom of
God is on the way. This hope is our motivation for
all our work on behalf of the gospel; any progress we
make stems from it.

This means that our practical activity should never
be our chief concern. The worldly – and the world's
religions – appear to be powerful and successful. We,
on the other hand, are weak and easily pushed into a
corner. Yet who is on firmer ground (1 Cor. 1:18–31)?

God's kingdom works in strange ways. Where is there a church, congregation, race, nation, or even a single person manifesting the kingdom of God today? Yet the kingdom of God is astir under the surface and spreads in new ways (Matt. 13:31–33). Now, more than ever, we must proclaim, "The Lord is at hand!" We are part of this, quietly and actively, through our faith and expectation. It is enough for us to know that God is weaving his design in the warp and weft of the world. His goal will be reached, not just for this or that person, but for everyone.

Where will the kingdom of God come from? Is not the entire history of the world a fulfillment of the promise? Are not bonds loosed, chains broken asunder? Who would have thought, for example, that new paths could open up for women as they have for men? Jesus lives, and he conquers more and more, although too many of us are unaware that he is behind it all. Of course, these developments do not of themselves represent a turning toward God, yet this practical liberation enables God's kingdom to break in among the people.

Only a very few people have a true and living hope for God's intervention. But there is a growing

# Plough Quarterly FREE TRIAL ISSUE

A bold, hope-filled magazine to inspire faith and action.

Each issue features interviews, stories, book reviews, and poetry on a core theme such as peacemaking, children and family, church community, biblical justice, the environment, or simple living.

☑ **Yes! Please send me** my free trial issue of *Plough Quarterly*. If I like it, I'll pay just $18 for 4 more issues (5 issues in all). I save **44%** off the $32 regular rate. As a subscriber I'll also get a free digital subscription and free access to dozens of Plough ebooks.

**No cost, no obligation.** If I decide not to subscribe, I'll simply write "cancel" on the invoice, return it, and owe nothing. Either way, the trial issue is mine to keep.

Name in print
_____

Address
_____

City _____ State _____ Zip _____

Phone number
_____

E-mail (We will not share your email address with any third party)
_____

Please allow 4–6 weeks for delivery of your free issue. No need to send money now; we will bill you later. You can also call 800-521-8011 or go to **www.plough.com/dmspecial.**

**B15BK**

# BUSINESS REPLY MAIL

FIRST–CLASS MAIL    PERMIT NO. 332    CONGERS, NY

POSTAGE WILL BE PAID BY ADDRESSEE

PLOUGH QUARTERLY
PO BOX 345
CONGERS NY 10920–9895

movement of the Spirit that runs throughout the world, and you must give yourself to it. The world is experiencing an immense transformation, and everything is being shaken up. And yet in the background there are quiet but powerful currents of peace, grace, and goodwill among people. God strides forward. The hidden Christ is at work (John 1:9). Keep this before your eyes! We are in the background, but our prayers, our faith, and our hope all play a part. Clearly, our lives should show that we must decrease, and he increase (John 3:30).

**The kingdom of God** has little in common with the world's religions. God only reveals himself as the one, holy God through the deeds of the Spirit, which no amount of piety or learning can replace. Our hope lies in the fact that Jesus, the son of God, lives *in* the world, not above it, even if he remains inconspicuous.

The Risen One wants to draw *all* people to himself (John 12:32), and so propaganda for a particular confession of faith or church is no concern of his. You must stand up and represent the gospel of the kingdom that shines for all people, no matter who they are.

Never forget that Jesus comes from and for the lowly; it is from their vantage point that he will illuminate the world (Luke 4:17–19). The expectation of redemption, the healing of societies and nations, the longing for God to bring about his heavenly kingdom on earth, the hope that the masters of capital will cease treating the masses as slaves – all this will unite us with the hearts of the humble and downtrodden. They especially will understand what we mean by God's kingdom, even if they have never sought him.

As I see it, God's wrath is sweeping over the Christian West precisely because a proud culture and pious Christianity have been pushed onto the people, while at the same time they are despised. To forget that all of us belong to God – whether pagan or Christian – is hardhearted and dishonest. The whole of Western civilization is tainted, much as the Romans were with their Caesars, regarding the rest of the world as dirt or as an opportunity for exploitation.

How can this go on? God must intervene and open our eyes; that is the only help I know of. The ruling prince of this world should not be allowed any more victories (1 John 3:8). He has trampled emerging humankind into the muck a hundred times already. He must no longer be allowed to do this.

**4**

**In seeking God's kingdom** you must also seek his righteousness, his justice, and build on an economic foundation, not just a spiritual one (James 2:14–17). For it is on the material plane that Jesus is victorious on earth. The devil laughs up his sleeve at all our religious meetings and theology. Spiritual communities that fail to be a corrective in everyday life and practical work will soon end in a fiasco, be they Buddhist or Christian. There must be absolutely no Christian pretense, however religious it may appear, for lots of religious activity deprives people of their true life. People need to be guided properly through practical work, not through the might of weapons or proselytizing or religious fervor.

Someday, when God's kingdom conquers the earth, true piety will infuse hands-on activity and work (Eph. 4:28). For unity between people can only come about on the foundation of communal life. Think more deeply about this. In God's kingdom, Christian churches are done for, since they have become little more than egotistical worlds consisting of personal concerns that keep people apart. The misery of the masses can only be alleviated by forming associations of people who live by the Holy Spirit and freely lend practical help to one another. This, in the end, is the surest way to influence those in power. A people's community that accomplishes something on the practical level will gain respect and authority among those who don't believe (Acts 2:44–47).

This may shock you, but we must preach that religious knowledge by itself is of no value. People should learn how to be truly active, especially with their neighbors, and to see to it that all have what they need to live a fruitful life. We need to keep the true goal in mind: the need of the world and the benefit of the people. That is the mind and spirit of Christ who reconciles all things. This is what we mean by seeking first the kingdom of God.

**It is a strange matter,** all this talk about everlasting life. To be honest, I don't trust those who always console people by pointing them to eternity. If we can't see any of God's help in *this* world, who can guarantee that there will be help in the next? Or did the Savior concern himself only with some heavenly realm? No! He came to *us* and dwelt among us. He showed us that the misery on earth will be eliminated once the barriers between time and eternity, between here and beyond, have been broken down. Through Christ a hole has been broken through from above down to us, not the other way around. So be on your guard. Today's Christianity has made all kinds of holes out of this world, falsely teaching that we can simply fly out of it, like pigeons, and be saved.

I know this will sound strange to many Christian ears, and even to those with whom you work. But what is the truth according to the Bible: our death and some afterlife, or the future of God's kingdom on the earth? The Bible, from its first to its last chapter, deals with the coming of God into this world. There is virtually nothing about dying and the next world. The Bible guarantees to us the deeds of God, here and now, where you and I live (Matt. 4:23–25).

**There's a lot of talk** about the world's dire social conditions and the needs that are all around us. It's amazing to think how many people still dream of a world in which there is true peace. Of course they are right to do so. But if the One who made the world and has our lives in his hand is not acknowledged, if we refuse to turn to him as the power and Lord we need for this, this dream is but a fantasy. Nothing will come of it. Set up governments based on the various opinions of outstanding leaders who believe they have the answer. Let one be based on a communistic ideal; let one operate according to some benevolent, supreme authority, perhaps with a religious framework; or have one in which only the poor, the underclass, have anything to say, and nobody else. Pass as many laws as you like; you will still see the same awful mess we are in today. Apart from God's rulership we remain inwardly and outwardly unclear and cannot form a society of truth and justice.

The greatest obstacle to the kingdom of God, therefore, is not our social conditions but is in us and in our clever solutions. It is self-will that leads people to destruction (Rom. 1:18–32). In this regard, our Christian organizations are not very helpful. Much too much pride has crept into them. Unless we arrive at the point where we dispel the foggy atmosphere of human effort and humanly devised ideals, unless we confront our ego-driven lives and look clearly at ourselves and say, "Without Jesus, we are nothing," we are lost (John 15:5).

**Remember,** there is no other purpose in your mission work than to proclaim God's kingdom and bring it to the people (Matt. 10:5–42). Take your stand, therefore, with faith, courage, and perseverance. God's kingdom *will* come. Rather lose your life than give up this goal! Boldly persist and keep this divine end uppermost in your mind, so that those you work with may experience how God makes things right. Live in God's splendor. Of course, this won't happen unless you want it.

Will we preach a "heavenly" Christ for another two thousand years? What's the use? Preach a "church" Christ? A "community" Christ? A "consoling" Christ? No good either. The renewal of this world will not happen. You must represent the living Christ who brings forth God's justice on the earth. Keep seeking God's kingdom in the love of Christ, and you will witness redemption in even the smallest matters. If you strive for God's justice in the name of all who suffer, not just for a few, redemption will come.

**2**

# Avoid Being Religious

**So much missionary work** is now superfluous. I will
put it even more strongly: most current missionary
endeavors are dangerous, because they self-righ-
teously attack the moral sensibilities and customs
of the unbelieving. Western Christians have become
the supreme moralists. But what do the "lost ones"
among us really want? People everywhere are occu-
pied with the question: How should we live our lives
on this earth? But it's no wonder they don't expect
any answers from religion. They even dread our
Christian ideas, for instead of giving strength to live,
they discourage; instead of freeing, they bind.

Our Christianity is not a living witness to the power
of the truth, which could, if God's rulership mattered
to us, overcome the various values of this world, even
honorable ones like those of Confucianism and Islam.
Instead, our churches are shot through with so many

empty, irrelevant customs and practices that they stand no higher in God's eyes than those of the pagans (Rom. 14:13–22). We fall far short of the glory we should have before God. But let us quietly hope that the unbelieving world is not forever lost in its unbelief, nor that we Christians are forever steeped in our Christianity. Let us look for something new – a life in God through Christ and the Spirit.

**Behind so many** of our current missionary and outreach efforts lies some kind of powerful organization. Consequently, a certain kind of worship of God is assumed, which is crushing and dogmatic. Our whole Christian system, with all its forms, lacks respect for different cultures and ways of being. It can be compared to a house all spick-and-span and ready for people to move into. It is a house of tranquil conscience; those who take up residence there feel quite secure and content with themselves – and yet they incur God's judgment.

You, however, should rejoice because your work does not depend on such an organization. You should have only the gospel in your heart, which flees all the trivial disputes that bog Christians down. You are in a foreign land armed only with the gospel, almost like it was for the very first Christians. Rejoice! The first Christians remained neither Jews nor Greeks; they did not rely on elaborate customs or traditions (Gal. 3:26–28). They were regarded as outlaws because of Christ. May it be the same with us!

Those in power will not concern themselves with us, for the powers that be cannot really grasp what we are about. Even the most beneficial things we do are of no value to them. Such things do not serve their ideas of a strong state or nation. Our activities cannot be incorporated into any official government department (Luke 22:24–30). My serious plea to God is that our work in the name of Christ remains free and may be given concrete expression, for everything born of the Spirit must have a visible body if it is to remain alive.

Our faith demands commitment and account-ability. God's people must not just live for the moment, but must have something lasting to hold on to, something to which they can remain faithful. Yet this is nothing we humans can plan or create.

Keep this in mind when you think about trying to start some kind of association. Such a group could be a small opening for God to work in the hearts of the people, but only if it is closely knit and affords you the opportunity to further witness to God's reign. Your utmost desire should be that hope for God's kingdom awakens in people's hearts. A group or fellowship in which the characteristics of Christ are alive is in fact a "church" (Acts 2:42). May God grant you such an abundance of his spirit that those around you are gripped by Christ and his true nature.

**How can one gain** a foothold in non-Christian cultures today? Certainly not by starting a Christian organization or a "mission station," to use the language of missionaries. If you were to do this the message of Jesus would be "foreign," something imported from elsewhere, not something that springs from native soil (which it always does). For this reason, any efforts to recruit or advertise could put your work on a human foundation and undermine the future of Christ where you are.

Remember, stay in reach of the people near you. God can send out his spirit and his word as far as he wants from some small spot. There is certainly no need for you to be everywhere at once. God's thoughts and God's will can spread out like ripples from even a single individual, and people can arrive at new ideas and deeds on their own without there always having to be a pastor behind it (1 Thess. 1:4–10). There is no telling where you would be if you were to follow the manner of thinking common among missionaries. Then the churches, especially in America, would be right in wanting to send a thousand missionaries to China and who knows where else, to convert the people. But that is sheer foolishness.

**We are not asked to do** anything spectacular. We are entrusted with the task of quietly giving the light of Christ's spirit and God's love to a world of human need. No storm can extinguish this light, a light that no darkness can overcome.

Therefore, do your utmost to understand the needs of the people and to learn how and where they can best be met (1 Thess. 2:7–12). The principle of mutual understanding between people, with their different needs and circumstances, is what will put an end to social strife and religious rivalries and jealousies. Until now religions, with their different concepts of

God, have been a source of division. But a faith that brings mutual respect will become a source of peace. This is why you must never engage in religious propaganda. Instead, regard every person as a child of God, equal to every other person and to yourself.

In this sense, it would be good to withdraw from the traditional role of a pastor or missionary. These roles are not from God but from men. To do something in the name of a position or title is not at all the same as doing it in the name of Jesus. Therefore, be on guard against the leaven of proselytizing. Remain on the same level with each person you meet. Changing hearts is not your business. God's spirit will do this according to his will, if only you stand rightly before him in your daily life.

Rejoice when, without any religious additions or trappings on your part, people feel from you something of Jesus, the Man of God's power. Yes, they can enter the kingdom of God without knowing how, only because they surrender themselves to the influence of the Spirit which is felt through your work. It is not your work, of course, but the work of God.

Millions are sighing, and Christ will come to them, bringing the kingdom of heaven. We must wait for

God's time, being completely aware that our goal is to bring the world into God's hands, not ours.

**People think that Jesus** was the founder of a new religion. But that is not God's Word to the world; his aim was not to give us a new religion or to help us live a bit more decently. He is the renewer of life (John 10:10). When Jesus spoke, it was a social matter. He proclaimed and brought forth the cause of God among us; he announced the inauguration of a new society, free of violence, hatred, and misery. He proclaimed the end of this world, where families are no longer able to be formed, where fathers don't know how to treat their children, where friendships are formed and then torn apart, where lives are lived in heartache. Jesus proclaimed: "The kingdom of God is at hand. Repent! You belong to God, not to these manmade structures of yours. You belong to God! Don't let yourself be oppressed by sin, greed, hatred, and immorality. Arise! You are a child of God." That is the gospel. Your loyalty, therefore, must only be to this gospel, to work that God himself enters this miserable, lost world.

I find it incomprehensible that people who call themselves devout believers consider themselves better than other people and separate themselves from "sinners." Jesus entered right into our human condition with all its ugliness. He united with people; he did not separate himself from the masses (Heb. 2:14–18). There are hundreds of thousands of people who seek to do the good and honest thing but who rightly refuse to go to church or have anything to do with religion. This happens because so many Christians stand above others. This world has had enough of that.

**I pray that those you work among** are led onto the right path – a free and godly path, not that of church or dogma. Then, with their own culture and language, they will be brought into the future unity of God's kingdom. For this reason, let the people develop at their own pace in economic and political matters, according to the times they live in. Whatever is necessary from God will come of itself, without our meddling.

Your being a pastor will gradually become more and more irrelevant. Every prophet, every

prophetically active person, will become "political,"
for seeking the kingdom of God leads into the world
of the people. If God gives you their hearts so that
they trust you, then they will come under his rulership, even without being called Christians. In fact,
it is harder to lead people out of the swamp of their
Christianity than out of the barbarity of sin and
unbelief (Matt. 23). After all, so many Christians have
become nothing more than whitewashed barbarians
living in self-deception. So don't be afraid of being
called a heathen among heathen, as long as you are
living in harmony with the spirit of God.

The intellectual and spiritual striving of most religious leaders has left the material life of the people
in the night of helplessness and sin. The world has
been dragging along, with no shortage of education,
and just as much moral decay. But this is a new time.
The spirit of truth, the righteousness of the kingdom,
seeks to enter into material, political, social, and
industrial life. God seeks to lay the foundation for
genuine knowledge. Politics, and all that goes with it,
must submit to the will of God.

God's kingdom takes hold of the earth. His way is
to establish the practical, material side of life first;

then spiritual life takes effect. This way puts solid ground under our feet, without which our efforts at spiritual work can have no effect and only place us at the mercy of every wind that blows. A spiritual framework must come into being, but it must come out of the natural life of the people; then the good news of God's rulership can be preached with a strength that puts it into practice.

**Unless you establish a base** among the people – outside of church and state and independent of institutions of coercion – Christ's kingdom will never advance. Sadly, what we have now is a massive human organization, without any divine support. Both the church and the state are riddled with gaping holes, and the people fall through. Nothing helps them.

Our Western Christianity is in a terrible mess. The church is tolerated only because it is the prop of the state and the broader culture. Together, they have become the "ruler of this world," with God reduced to an ornament for those in power. No one raises any real protest. People cling desperately to the old, ruined world, while the ruling powers view a new world as a threat. Individual freedom is thrust aside, and only those who allow themselves to be molded like dough can succeed.

The main thing, then, is to find an opening for the Spirit to work. We must not represent a theology or a church tradition; we simply need to draw near to people in the spirit of truth (Acts 10). God will lead you wisely, so that you do not need to pay homage to Christian superstition. Future developments are not our concern – the future is in God's hands, and developments will take place in his time. So take courage. The Prince of Peace will be victorious in China, Europe, and everywhere else!

We must each fight this battle, since we have all been shackled by Christianity's demonic power structure and the dominance of religious forms, which suppress the spirit of the true gospel. The Christ of the kingdom is still being crucified. The prince of this world is happy to have a "Christ" of the churches (those "temples built by human hands") to help him subjugate the people. We must overcome this lie by proclaiming the divine Word in patience and faith. It is good that time is on our side in this struggle; we need only hold out and remain true to what we have understood of God.

**In your work,** be careful not to exclude everything religious. It is quite right to say (as I myself have said many times) that the gospel is proclaimed by what we do. But the gospel demands that we always honor Jesus on earth. If we stay silent, how will he be honored (Rom. 10:14–15)? You need to help people realize that there is something better than human wisdom – even all the wisdom of Confucius (1 Cor. 2:2–5). At every opportunity we must confess to Jesus Christ and no other.

If you fail to offer any biblical instruction it will become increasingly apparent that something is missing. To be sure, one needs to develop a proper framework for instructing anyone in the faith, unveiling the kingdom of God upon earth using biblical stories (Acts 28:23–31). We can speak of the emergence of the one God of heaven and earth into the consciousness of certain individuals, the prophets, who witnessed God's glory and gave testimony to it (2 Pet. 1:19–21). Beginning with the creation, and then turning to God's struggle with the idolatrous and superstitious ideas and tendencies of humanity, we can lead on through the history of Israel, making use of the most beautiful and purest passages from the Law and the Prophets.

Then, with Jesus, a more intimate glimpse of God opens up (Heb. 1:1–3), and God the Almighty becomes the Father of all people. This is the gospel message: You are not a result of chance, but you belong to God, the one Lord of all. Therein lies the foundation for the new law of love. It is the forgiveness of sins and love for all people. Any morals you happen to discuss and teach must therefore be connected to Jesus' life, which is focused solely on God's coming reign.

Avoid, however, turning the Bible into a historical curiosity or some kind of spiritual manual. The scriptures have something meaningful to say to us about God and his will for the earth. Take the Old Testament account of the Israelites' exodus from Egypt, for example: the essential point is the miracle that enabled the Israelites to become a people, and how particular prophets among them gave witness to God. The details are there in order to support *this* truth. Or, take the case of Lazarus in the New Testament (John 11). Here the central point is Jesus' claim: "I am the resurrection and the life." It is this momentous proclamation that frames the events surrounding Lazarus. The truth that Jesus has risen and is alive is the heart of what has to be said.

The greatest truth of the Bible is that God revealed himself in Jesus. Jesus is the one to whom the prophets point (1 Peter 1:10–12). This ultimately should be the focus of your work, be it in deed or word. We dare not be silent about the divine powers present in the person of Jesus, standing before us like great promises and bringing hope into our lives. The importance of Jesus must be gleaned from the entire Bible so that he is in the center, always alive and decisive in all the changing circumstances of the world.

**A movement of the Spirit** will never come from having religion – especially not from church rectories and parsonages. The institutional churches, in their so-called wisdom, too often use their power to crush the free stirring of the Spirit, or at best ignore it. Of course, this is not so everywhere. In many places you find joy in a gospel that respects human beings, a message that does not crush people but stems from God's character-building love.

Keep this gospel in your heart, and it will bear fruit. Your experiences will give the seed of the kingdom more freedom to germinate and grow. Simply stand alongside Jesus Christ, the only mediator between God and humankind. Root out that middleman in you who has crept in between, so that you can approach every person not as clergy, but as a disciple and slave of Christ. If you are to preach anything, proclaim the rulership of God, and do so despite the roaring and raging of the world.

**The typical Western view** of Christianity is that we fight to carve out a path for the gospel, even in the name of "justice." The inconsistency of today's Christian church is as crass as at the time of the crusades, when people were "converted" at sword-point. Protect the people who have yet to believe from the pious Christians who judge them. Don't look left or right, but follow after Christ, the Savior of all people.

It breaks my heart that there is so much nationalism and violence in the name of Christ. European Christians have brought a curse upon their own heads by killing so many other peoples. Judgment has come upon Christianity because it lacks the strength to love its enemies. The salt has lost its savor and is of no use.

All this goes to show how "civilized people," or our modern culture, cannot understand Christ. Sadly, the majority of missionary societies are no different.

Businessmen, church workers, the military – all in their own way want to put people into their own pocket, instead of into God's hands. Furthermore, the numerous denominations and Christian sects, with all their different creeds and ideas, are one of the greatest hindrances to Christ. They fail to understand that in him, God has reconciled the whole world (2 Cor. 5:19–21).

**I am very glad** that you are befriending your neighbors, and I hope very much that you win their hearts. I am also happy that you are working with the sick and destitute. Even if many people's deeds are evil, God's fatherly hand will bring about good things again.

But no one should become Christian according to our formula. May God grant you the baptism that is in accord with his will, not ours, so that people become truly free and liberated. Whether they are called Christians or not is in the end immaterial – despite what many churches seem to think.

Churches and sects too easily create nothing but stumbling blocks by organizing congregations and emphasizing baptisms. This is totally out of place in these last days of God's advancing kingdom. I actually wonder if there hasn't been a misunderstanding right from the beginning, when large groups were baptized. Perhaps when Peter said, "Can anyone keep these people from being baptized with water?" (Acts 10:47) after Cornelius had received the Spirit's baptism, he should simply have said, "Why bother with water at all when the Spirit is present?" Likewise, when Jesus said, "Go forth and make all nations my disciples; baptize people everywhere" (Matt. 28:19), it seems obvious to me that he was emphasizing the Spirit's baptism, not of getting people into water.

The communion you have with the people, in the way Jesus intended, will lead them to trust you so that you in turn can teach them. This will bring about real baptism – baptism of the Spirit. Perhaps later on, a church baptism by water will follow. But I ask you to look upon all who come to you in trust as your sheep, or rather as Christ's, and to make no distinctions on the basis of water baptism. In fact, avoid having to choose whom you baptize. Let them all be entrusted to you; then God can increase and deepen his authority over wide areas, and thousands will be able to discover the heavenly Father according to the

Spirit given them. Then their idols will collapse of themselves.

Your aim should be to reach the people, not just those who want to be baptized. Unfortunately, so many zealous missionaries prefer to pursue the stupid idea of establishing officially recognized local churches – a glory to men for sure, but an insult to God – instead of bringing the gospel to the people. They prefer a false piety that limits God to saving individuals, but not the world itself. My counsel is to go slowly, without a lot of words and without a lot of discussion of Christian principles.

You are standing at a critical juncture in God's history, so don't fall into institutional ways of organizing church services or mission outposts. Believe me, as soon as you start baptismal services you will attract flatterers and profit seekers, and then God will withdraw his sheep. Strive to become one with the people, even if this leads you away from those who think along ecclesiastical lines.

Do you understand what I mean? God will open new doors and prepare new vessels (Acts 2:17–21), because the Spirit will not remain in old wineskins.

**Much of Christianity's** history shows what an error it is to rely too much on the sacraments. People are baptized, confirmed, blessed, consecrated at the altar, and then as if it were all nothing, they run off and join up with the nearest available blabbermouth and impostor. The sacraments are not glue to hold a community together. On the contrary, the more intensively they are promoted, the further we are from God's intervention.

In this sense, I see water baptism as a necessary evil. I personally long for some other means by which people can join Christ's body. No outward form can bring this about; it must be given by the Spirit (Gal. 6:15). Those who place such importance on outward symbols end up thinking they are superior. If you begin to emphasize this one outward act of baptism, then people will surely rush to join you – but they will run off again just as quickly. You must see it as Jesus did, who even had to ask his own disciples, "Do you wish to go away too?" (John 6:67).

You and I know that the only way we can gain a broader vision is through faith. If God is restricted to gathering people through the typical means we have seen so far, then his kingdom is lost (John 10:16). Jesus is not a lifeless idol! He is life, and he is constantly moving forward from the old to the new. Critical times will come and everyone will be in danger of deserting the true Jesus. To be baptized a hundred times over will not prevent this. One must be of the same spirit as Jesus.

Recall how the apostles fought for the fledgling churches; it did not help them one bit that they baptized three thousand in one day. Far too many, in those first years, failed to remain faithful. Thus hard things had to be written, as in the Letter to the Hebrews (Heb. 6).

Never forget: "God so loved the world . . . " (John 3:16). It is actually a miracle that you can associate with unbelievers in the name of Christ without having to get them baptized and into some church. After all, too often the baptism of the churches divides Christians from the rest of humankind. God's spirit must flow from heaven down to earth without pious human means. His spirit compels people to do what is needed – even if they are not aware of doing it – so that in the end they will say, "Lord, when have we served you?" (Matt. 25:37–40). Yes, even today there is a great deal of work going on for the kingdom of God outside of the walls of the church, and people are not aware of it.

**Again, regarding the matter of baptism,** take the spirit of what I have said – it should never be a matter of principle – and then act freely in individual cases. It seems to me that your situation may be similar to the apostle Paul's, to whom baptism was unimportant (1 Cor. 1:14–17). He left it to others. I am glad that you are doing the same. We must not despise conventional church practices, just as Jesus did not despise the custom of sacrifice, but our aim is to step into the new world. The time will come when God's baptism is only in the Spirit. "Yet a time is coming and has now come when the true worshipers will worship the Father in the spirit and in truth, for they are the kind of worshipers the Father seeks" (John 4:23).

In the meantime, it does not matter if you bless some individuals or baptize them, as long as they do not think this gives them the right to judge others. That is the main point I am driving at: it is not the outward practice *per se* that is harmful but the arrogance, pride, and separation from others that too often follow in its wake. In contrast, God's baptism of the Spirit makes us brothers with all people. Be sure to tell this to those you work with when the opportunity arises. Then they can be baptized in God's name, by him.

It may happen that converts come to you and request baptism. If they do this of their own accord and with pure motives, then follow the example of Jesus' disciples and baptize them. There is a difference between us going out to get converts and individuals coming to us with the desire to make public their allegiance to Christ. Still, our business is not to promote religious practices but to teach and love. People should know that we labor in Christ and that we will never hinder anyone from joining another group of Christians.

To say it again: whatever you do, don't let ecclesiastical matters cause separation – the "holy" on one side, the "unholy" on the other. Rather, let all you do be a quiet act of prayer. Allow yourself to be led quite freely (Gal. 5:25–26). Then you will know what is important at a given moment. I pray that you remain a genuine messenger of God, proclaiming his love for the lost. His love belongs to the unbeliever just as much as it does to Christians.

**Why is it so hard** for people to imagine anyone coming to God without walking through church doors? If only we would realize that we are at a stage in God's history when, through hearts yearning for freedom, God will reveal his justice. It will spell the end of human laws and rights, and people will know in their hearts what is right and what is wrong. God wants to bring this about. We who bear his image must learn what is required of us as true men and women. Religion has never supplied this and never will.

What, then, is the character of God's church? Certainly it is not a matter of being bound in uniformity through religious rites (Gal. 3:1–5). The people of God's spirit are joined together in much the same manner as scientists whose love of knowledge and shared interests draw them together. Each brings his own unique experience and perspective, and works and studies in his own characteristic way, while always keeping in mind the efforts of all. This is how we too should function. Our goal is a united fellowship whose members appreciate and love one another and place Jesus above all else.

**Many people never really consider** why they are Christians. So much gets preached besides the true gospel, which is that God wants to remake humanity, so that the *earth* – not just heaven – might be filled with his glory. But too many Christians are content with a Christ of religion. Like pagans, they look for happiness after death. They relinquish the earth, and thereby themselves and other people. Their only interest is a blessed assurance in death, not the kingdom of God on earth.

If Christians think that people have to be just like them in order to find consolation at the end of their lives, we must protest: No! There were plenty of people who died consoled before Christ came. That is not why he came into the world. He came to create new men and new women (2 Cor. 5:17). Right here, on this earth, God wants to see his truth, justice, and love glorified. Only when this happens will we prove ourselves to be fully human.

God seeks to redeem humanity. But this redemption is a far cry from human achievement. As long as there are people, there will always be great works. Certainly in our day much is being achieved, but the driving force is little more than self-interest.

Recently I heard about missionaries in Samoa. What they encountered is truly remarkable. People live there from day to day, almost without thinking, but joyful and happy. The land and the trees belong to everyone, and no one has worries; they are content with one another. But now the mission wants to introduce private property. The Christians want to sell the land and teach the people how to compete and become ambitious for material gain, and thus wake them up so that Western culture can more easily be established there. Human achievements are introduced as if the only things that mattered were the works of our modern culture.

I say leave the people alone! Let them flourish in their simplicity. They don't have to become like us; they don't have to be as untruthful as we are. For in spite of all the material splendor we are living in now, countless lies run through our society and weigh us down completely.

Yes, people in material need should be helped – but God's love in them is already far stronger than all our lies! Our task is to "put on the new self" (Col. 3:9–11). If we strive to do this, and if the boredom of our theology and our Christianity has not already killed us, we can become people truly enthusiastic for Jesus. If Christ alone is our light and life, then we can possibly be of some help to those who don't believe. But religious talk is useless (Matt. 7:21). So is forming some kind of religious community where everyone sits together in a corner and prays and reads the Bible. No, make an effort to get rid of the lies that darken this world. Do this by endeavoring to live with an upright heart, in the power of God's truth.

**God will always** call individuals to him, regardless of how people in general think and organize themselves. He can cause life to flourish anywhere he chooses. That is why divine life can still blossom from the seedbed of the churches.

Nevertheless, we still need to devote ourselves to something brand new, something that opens a door and shows a way forward for entire peoples and nations. Once people are on the right path, they can acquire further understanding of divine things. The conversion of individuals is only a temporary measure. Individual conversion by itself risks the sin of pharisaism. A single converted person can so easily flatter himself, thinking he is now a special person able to give others a spiritual kick now and then.

We want to cast one net over all – over the good and evil, righteous and unrighteous, poor and rich, Christian and non-Christian – and then leave it to

God's unifying spirit to change, sift, and direct hearts (Matt. 13:47–52). Perhaps this is what Jesus meant by baptizing the people. They will come like captives into the kingdom of God, though most likely they will not even notice what is happening to them. And then they will find life.

So guard against the insolence of Christians who have no consideration for the cultural context they find themselves in. These Christians should bow before what God has already done. For example, it was Confucius who saw that reverence is the beginning of true worship. Each of us should have this same reverence, even for our enemies. So don't let the spirit of self-righteousness have the slightest chance of poisoning you, even from a distance.

# 3

# See How Christ Is Already at Work

**If you are observant,** you can always find traces of God
at work (Acts 17:23). God is always moving, in our
hearts and among those nearest to us. But if you get
too engrossed in what *you* are doing, you will not be
able to notice what God is trying to accomplish, just
as many did not see the working of God in the Savior.
So, keep your eyes and ears open, and as soon as you
perceive something of God's work, let it speak to you.

If you focus solely on all the need and suffering
that is before you, you will soon find yourself
groaning and lamenting like the Israelites in the
desert. Remember, God in his great mercy gave us
a new birth, "into a living hope by the resurrection of Jesus Christ from the dead" (1 Pet. 1:3). That
is the greatest event that has ever happened – the
resurrection – and the living hope within our hearts
is its consequence. With this hope, everything puts

on a different appearance, and we can confidently proclaim God's works and deeds.

**Some trace,** something very tangible, of Jesus Christ runs through all ages (Acts 14:16–17). Our distress is not that there is absolutely nothing to be seen of God in this world, but that the fleshly pursuits of this world seem to tower over the few small indications of God's spirit, that the vanity of this world, the perishable and the corruptible, seem to have the upper hand over the victory Jesus won on the cross. Even so, something of God's peace, which comes from the risen Savior, is always present. Hang on to this, come what may.

**God is always at hand;** he despises no one. If a heart shows itself to be only a little bit receptive, God is able to do something and reveal himself as the Living One who is present (Mark 7:24–30). He does not hesitate to approach anyone. At the time of Socrates, Plato, and Aristotle, God revealed himself, though naturally according to the context of their time (Rom. 1:18–21). Despite the whole outlook of that period of history – when for example slavery was considered essential, as it was even in the time of the apostles – God revealed himself in such a living way that we, in our time, still draw on it. God was even able to reveal his glory in the brutality of the people of Israel, at the time of the conquest of the land, and later among the kings.

So it is that God continues to speak today. He frees us again and again from old conceptions. So look for how God is at work. Though today people think that this or that idea is absolutely impossible, by tomorrow they are very likely to think quite differently. Recall what a tremendous struggle there was against the abolition of slavery. Today, however, slavery is deemed inhuman. Therefore, don't cling tightly to anything or despair over how things are (Col. 2:20). God will put an end to everything that does not belong in his kingdom.

**God is at work everywhere,** but not in the same way. The origin and development of what we call culture or civilization remains a mystery. Why has it taken root more in some countries and peoples than in others?

In general, the active spiritual and intellectual life of a people comes from God, who brings about human development. This happens all over the world.

Though God has let nations go their own way, "he has not left himself without testimony" (Acts 14:16–17). Without this witness, we would remain on the same level as animals. The Spirit brings about spiritual history, rooted in a continual struggle for God's kingdom. I am sure that this is the case in every civilization.

God's plan is to lift us out of our animal-like existence into the life of the Spirit. A great deal of truth still has to be revealed – from non-Christian peoples as well – to show that from the beginning God has wanted to create something good and true wherever there is an opening, far beyond our narrow boundaries.

Still, I purposely do not refer to "divine revelation" when describing so-called high culture. Cultural manifestations in general remain on a lower level, developing and growing and then dying off. When God reveals himself something altogether different takes place: humankind recognizes its immortal nature, its eternal destiny. The truth shines through, and the temporal developments that once seemed all-important are cut down to size.

God's revelation bursts forth again and again as a pure ideal, in the midst of the most frightful confusion of events. "You are of this world; I am not of this world," Jesus said (John 8:23). God is, of course, in this world. What is transient and perishable – and alive for a time – is not possible without God. Yet it is not to be confused with the love that God puts into our hearts. Therefore, learn to distinguish between those active powers that produce culture or civilization, which God has a hand in, and divine revelation, which leads to the recognition of God's love.

**Death and damnation** certainly hold sway, the work of the "murderer from the beginning" (John 8:44). Nevertheless, people long to escape all this death. This longing comes from God. Imperceptibly, Jesus can take hold of this longing. And he will do so – Jesus, who came not to damn but to save (John 12:47).

It is true that certain scripture passages regarding damnation cause difficulty. Yet the sternest warnings of Jesus are addressed to the devout, not to unbelievers and sinners (Matt. 23). In a similar way, God's wrath as described in the Old Testament is directed at those who were once close to God, but

**41**

then dishonored him. The hard words of Jesus are meant for the rich, not for the oppressed masses who are ignorant of his Word (Luke 6:20–26). Our indignation should be turned against the Pharisees and scribes of our day. It is against these that the wrath of God is directed, not against the common people.

For centuries people have been exploited, ruled over, and enslaved, and have had to fight for themselves. Governments and the establishment have persistently struck them down. Underneath, however, the oppressed remain people of character. It is to them that Jesus comes, and the high and mighty will tremble before the multitude that Jesus will gather (Luke 14:16–24). Stand firm in Christ, therefore, and be at peace with everyone as far as you are able. There is nothing you can do except to be present. But your presence will awaken deeds of God, and Jesus, the lion of Zion, will raise himself up and conquer this world.

**The teachings of Confucius,** which promote knowledge of the heart rather than a set of rules, seem to me to be as fitting a foundation for Christ and his kingdom as the Law of Moses.

Sadly, a focus on the wrath and damnation that God is supposed to wreak on the godless has spread among Christians. This is in direct contradiction to the love of God, which the New Testament so clearly teaches. We must be careful to respect and acknowledge anyone (including the "pagan") who is led by God, and whose reverence even for his enemies has become a quality of heart (Rom. 2:12–16).

Jesus said, "Do not think that I have come to abolish the Law and the Prophets; I have not come to abolish them but to fulfill them" (Matt. 5:17). When we come to a foreign land in the name of Jesus, we should thank God that a law or ethic already exists which can find fulfillment. Or do we think we have first to hammer the laws of Moses or Christian morals into people? This would be to stand above God, whose spirit was at work long before we Christians showed up (Acts 17:16–31).

You should have no misgivings about upholding certain foreign customs, especially those in which people show reverence for God's working in their history – even if God's name is left unspoken. Through this, you are creating relationships built on truth (1 Cor. 9:19–23). This free action on your part will speak far louder than any sermon you could give. To the extent that you do this, reverence for the Father of all fathers, the Creator of everything good that is found among people, will increase. No one can honor God without honoring what is already of God in people.

**Every culture** is bound by practices that paralyze the people, just as much as Christians who are in the church's clutches (Rom. 3:9). In China, for example, people are imprisoned by an inordinate veneration of the family and an overemphasis on superstition. All this prevents them from experiencing any real change. You will no doubt encounter great obstacles the more you draw close to people and move beyond superficial acquaintance.

Many missionaries feel this makes them right in wanting to use Christianity to uproot the national or cultural character of the people. But they will soon find out where that leads! If a nationalistic spirit is aroused, on either side, then all foreign elements will be swept away, and the Christians themselves will become enemies. Only those who act justly toward the people and represent their interests in the face of oppression will stand the test of Christ's love. You will have no easy time of it.

To begin with, your work should only have a quiet influence. As long as you don't make Western Christian customs compulsory, you will not arouse opposition, and this will work to your advantage. Avoid all religious provocation. Let Christ quietly work and comfort people through you; they will sense the difference between what you and others are trying to do. Aggressive attempts at evangelizing do not spring from the love of God, but from the spirit of business.

Take heart, and may God give his spirit to all you meet! Remember, they don't need to become "Christians" like us. This designation need not come up at all. Whoever does the will of God is a child of the kingdom of heaven, whether he takes his cue from Confucius, Buddha, Muhammad, or the Church Fathers. Christ is the only one who brings truth and life into people's lives. Everything is in his hands.

Every nation is equal before God. Before him, unbelievers and pagans count just as much as Christians. People of all descriptions are entering God's kingdom. They are coming to Christ, but not to

Christians. The vision of the Son of Man – representing compassion, social responsibility, and equality through the works of peace – is catching on among the so-called irreligious. Here is the entry point for Christ's spirit, which will encompass the whole earth.

The sign of the coming kingdom will be the true man, the true woman – not the Christian, Muslim, or Buddhist. Religious people can say what they like, but this will not hinder the burgeoning movement of people and nations toward a humanity that strives for higher goals. And though these goals may seem weak and incomplete, God will still protect and preserve them for a new future.

**On a recent visit to Cairo,** I had to preach at a local mission outpost there. I was made acutely aware of what a distortion it is to play Christianity like a trump card when we relate with Muslims, instead of simply allowing the Savior to speak through us. Islam is not so absolutely closed that the spirit of God is unable to work there. Certainly, these people will never become European Christians – not that they would gain anything by it if they did.

There is something very impressive about the worship of Allah in the Islamic faith. Not only are there few religious forms, but there is a heartfelt devotion to Allah, even in the midst of misfortune and despite a strict moral code. As a religion, Islam has the kind of strength that is able to influence the actions of its followers. It is true that in many ways Islam is quite rigid, which obscures the living, human, and personal love of our Father in heaven. Only Jesus, the Son of Man, can reveal this to them. But to the Muslim, we Christians appear immoral and irreligious – and not without some justification.

**Popular movements** in many places around the world demonstrate the urge in countless hearts to be done with old forms and worn-out practices that have no consequence in daily life. Indeed, a common characteristic of all such movements is the search for practical means to better people's lives. And even if this seeking remains on a secular level, God still speaks through these movements and their attempts at change.

When you read standard accounts of history, what stands out is the way key events are expressed in merely human terms, with no thought for God's hand at work. These accounts often contradict the spirit of God. We are by nature very slow to comprehend the working of the Spirit. Seen from our vantage point, a great deal of what we know of earlier events and times appears wicked and wrong. Instead, we should be looking for the points of light that have pierced, and do pierce, the dark night of human existence. God's spirit flares up repeatedly, albeit briefly and through imperfect instruments. With Moses, for instance, it was in the redeeming power of the Lord's name: "the compassionate and gracious God, slow to anger, abounding in love and faithfulness" (Exod. 34:5–7). With David it was in forgiveness: "Blessed is the one whose transgressions are forgiven" (Ps. 32:1). With Elijah it was in the terrible struggle against powers of darkness.

Where there is clear revelation from God, social, political, and even religious rules and regulations are forgotten (Col. 2:16–23). Though God's revelation comes to us through people's lives, ultimately only Jesus brings about what is new and pure. Political and religious forms and cultural mores are constantly changing; they belong to what is human and transitory. Christ's true followers never feel obligated to follow them.

Confucius, Buddha, and other great religious figures are not equal to Christ (Acts 4:12). A civilization like the Chinese – just as others in the course of human history – strives ultimately for a social order. Yet Confucius offers virtually nothing to quench our deepest thirst. A mere moral philosophy, however significant it may be, cannot lift us up to God.

Only Christ expresses God's nature clearly (John 14:6). Apart from him all our efforts to change society will collapse as soon as outer circumstances change. Christ must redeem us from "the curse of the law" (Gal. 3:13) that we may enter into "the freedom and glory of the children of God" (Rom. 8:21). It is the law and human morality that hold people back. As my father wrote to me when I was young, "Our virtues have become our greatest sin." They hinder the living God from bringing about something new.

Although profound outer changes can occur quite apart from any revelation from God, there is nothing more wonderful than the indwelling Christ. When he is present streams of living water flow out, bringing true life to people (John 4:13–14). This is something that transcends human goodness. What God directs is never destroyed, even when nations suffer ruin. Only where Christ's love rules are human beings valued for who they are, and everything else – social institutions and customs – takes second place and even becomes unimportant.

The hidden church of Jesus Christ, out of which something of God's future can come, remains and will never die. It is only the mantles of religion and philosophy and Christianity that are in tatters. A new mantle is needed – made of God's pure love and the capacity to receive it.

**Don't forget** that whatever good you may find within yourself must also lie hidden in other people. So never despise those around you in whom this goodness has not yet come to light. Believe in the people, even in those whose ideas and ways of life are completely the opposite of your own. Accept them as you do your-self. If you have faith, not only in God but in what lies buried within each person, then they will have faith too. If you seek God alone, then that which is from God in others will come alive, whether or not you can see it. Jesus sees what is of God in others, even if it is still hidden as a tiny seed.

This is the gospel you must proclaim. Preach it simply. Jesus values each person; he sees their dignity as God created them. He came to rid every person of shame and self-contempt, of the feeling that they are nothing and can do nothing, the feeling that they have ruined everything and nothing can change that, the feeling that all is hopeless. He came to assure the disheartened that they can still be reborn. Resurrection is possible again and again, in spite of all our weakness and sin, even if our bodies should perish.

There remains a precious jewel in every person, which is stronger than any outward pressure in their lives (John 1:9). It remains inviolable, even in those who feel that they are lost in their rottenness. No matter how badly they have ruined their lives, this jewel remains in them; it is as certain as that God was reconciling the world to himself in Jesus Christ. There is something in each person that will never be lost, something that can always be resurrected. That is the gospel.

**There are people** who stamp around in a rage and can't understand why any of us should continue living. They throw Christianity away. And yet beneath the surface, such people may actually possess a strong faith in God. They may call themselves "atheists" and even live ungodly lives, yet they are perhaps the closest to God. They long to truly live and have not yet given up hope. You will find that it is often secular thinkers, the irreligious, who muse most about the possibility of a new time, when everything can be set right. What about us? If we claim to believe the gospel, then why haven't we brought the *true life* to them? Why don't we live and work in the world as the light of life?

**Never before** have the laws of nature been as well understood as now. Never before have we known so much about the starry heavens. Never before has the earth been explored to the extent it is today. In the space of a few decades, our material lives have drastically changed. Don't disparage this, for it is partly the result of the Holy Spirit at work in this world.

Rejoice that certain weighty questions are now being raised which in past millennia were unthinkable: How can we really become human? How can we build mutual relationships that make life on earth tolerable for all people? How can peace be achieved among the nations? It is easy for us Christians to ridicule these kinds of questions. It is always easy to scoff. Our task, however, as witnesses of the gospel, is to take part in these questions. Think about it. After thousands of years the questions are now raised: How can we abolish war? How can we eliminate poverty? This comes from God. God is at work. These questions are good, and all good thoughts come from the Spirit. If people around the world are voicing them, we also need to speak up and contribute.

# 4

# **Remain among the People**

**When you come** to a strange village or to a new situation, never preach until you have a warm contact with the people there. For you must not be a stranger. First become known and win trust on the social and economic level. As the apostle Paul said, "To the Jews I became like a Jew, to win the Jews. . . . I have become all things to all people so that by all possible means I might save some" (1 Cor. 9:19–22). Only then should you preach, but still with caution. It is not our preaching but our life that must give people light. How shall they understand something of the kingdom of God if we speak to them of it before they have seen anything of it? Up to now the only kind of kingdom, or social order, they have seen has been one of violence and oppression. If you do not act in a different way and meet them on their own level as a friend, they will understand nothing of God's kingdom.

What should one do about customs such as the offering of sacrifices? You cannot abruptly brush off such customs (1 Cor. 10:23–11:1). After all, how different is it when we visit graves, decorate Christmas trees, or light candles? What is most important is that when a person seeks to be baptized he or she should prove that he is a child of God through his love, before offending those around him by abstaining from a national custom.

Instead of building upon spirit and love, Christian churches are too often built upon opposition to outward cultural customs. Did not the apostles also enter the temple, and did not Christians in many places partake of sacrificed foods (1 Cor. 8)? Such customs will only cease when the Spirit has permeated everything. Jesus went into every corner of the world of sin and trusted in the Spirit to make headway there. This is naturally much harder than founding a church that rejects a few customs and habits.

Our faith is founded on hope. The kingdom of God cannot be established everywhere now. It is only a hope (Rom. 8:22–25). What we have of it in our hearts must work quietly, bringing light to people without their knowing what is happening to them. Therefore, stand on the broad ground of the people and live and work among them, especially the poor, the spiritually undeveloped, the oppressed and despised. In so doing show them God's love. Do this even at the risk of being regarded as an infidel, as I have been. People who have their hearts in the right place will still come to us.

**I often ponder** over how Christ can be brought to the people in a foreign culture. It seems to me a head-on approach is fruitless; I would rather say Christ must come up behind people, so to speak. I feel that through Christ, God's rulership is taking hold in our day, but in such a way that we are unable to point out, "That is from Christ." Only at the end will we recognize that everything good that has been achieved has come from Christ and his spirit.

You can be sure that God already has a vast people in the country where you are. Your task is to remain and represent the gospel in its truest sense. You are not just in one town – you are in the whole country.

For Christ is not just in a certain place, but among
entire peoples. You are not representing a church;
you are an ambassador of the gospel (2 Cor. 5:20).
Hence, for the present it does not matter much what
you do – what matters is that you are there among the
people. Your life is hidden in Christ, so do not try to
compete with organized mission efforts.

You will certainly be in dialog with others who
share your own background, but in spirit you must
seek to be among the people. Blessed are the poor –
they will inherit the kingdom of heaven (Luke 6:20).
If you speak in this way, and of the love of God,
even your compatriots will understand it. This will
surely interest them far more than some catechism or
doctrinal statement. Your words will have spice, and
your preaching will have significance for everyone.

Be glad merely to stay in touch with the daily
goings-on of the people around you. Don't try to have
"religious" contact with them. They do not need to
become Christians at first – perhaps never. As I have
said many times, they may never call themselves
Christians, as we call ourselves, but simply children
of God. The spirit of God must come to meet you
from the midst of the people themselves, and this

will happen, because it is God's way. You are only a watchman. The people will come to recognize Christ through his spirit, and then theirs will be a true, divine Christianity, not a Westernized one.

**Today's missionaries** often make the grave mistake of acting like professors instructing students, while at the same time churches and Christian societies carry on like industrialists, measuring everything in terms of "success." We must do things differently and meet everyone on the same level, without criticism. Our task is to radiate divine love, teach by example, and respect all as fellow human beings (1 Thess. 2:1–16). This will demand time and much patient prayer, but the Savior, the Risen One, will open the doors.

Again, wait quietly; it will soon be clear to you what you must do. The true Christ must come, who addresses the questions of life. A true missionary should in the name of Jesus live and bring life, not religious debate. Genuine faith is built upon a people made alive by God, not the other way around.

For this reason don't study the people. Be natural with them and accept them as they are, but at the same time do not let them affect you wrongly. Have no agenda whatsoever. All of our human efforts and judging will only lead to complications. Be joyful, carefree, and single-minded. Be free in spirit, free in God, and free of opinions. Unite with people as God leads them to you, no matter who they are. The ninety-nine righteous ones will have to remain where they are, for the Savior seeks the one lost sheep (Matt. 18:10–14). Christ came into the flesh, and the world will experience that. So be a servant, not a master.

**What tremendous power** was experienced among the first apostles! (Acts 5:12–16) Gentiles, Jews, and Romans were united freely in one spirit (Eph. 2:11–22). The apostles, in the power of the Spirit, proclaimed to those who believed: You are slaves and yet are free; are Gentiles and yet belong to God; are free and yet bound to humankind! (Rom. 6:15–23) Where do we find this spirit of solidarity today?

Pray, therefore, for God to set you free. If through his grace the poor and the downtrodden flock to you, things will go forward of their own accord. You will find that there is power in the apostolic task among the working classes – I have never found such hungering for God anywhere else. Though their struggle to stay alive often leaves God and religious matters sidelined, they are nonetheless guided by him and bear in their hearts hope for the world's redemption.

By all means continue to minister to your fellow Christians. But whatever you do, don't shut out the people you are there for! "All those the Father gives me will come to me, and whoever comes to me I will never drive away" (John 6:37). Those are the words of the living Savior. The worthless, despised, and down-trodden will come to you when you allow Jesus to be with you.

**The working of God's spirit** does not hinge on the efforts of one person alone, but rather on the preparation of a people and place as a sanctuary for God. If you cannot find a footing among the people themselves, then your house will be built on sand. You must be among the people so that ultimately you can dispense with patronage (Acts 16:11–15). Rather remain lowly than be honored by government officials or successful businessmen.

The only true and genuine work in the Lord is hidden; it is a mystery. We must labor with much effort and sweat, even when no one understands what we are doing. People only value outward success, which is deadly. They want to do everything according to their own ideas. Rather than fighting for the coming of God's reign, they try to attack and overcome the world, all in the name of Christ. This is nothing but spiritual arrogance.

The outward successes of your faithful labor may indeed show signs of God's blessing, but do not let this distract you. We are striving for something much greater. Something new is quietly being prepared, and this must be completed. We can help, but only if we remain faithfully at the place where God is at work. We are nothing. Those who listen to us, in the end, will be the poor and wretched, not the high and mighty. I would not change places with any of the great on earth. So build only on the Rock, in order to be free of all those who are enamored with power and influence.

**Jesus welcomed sinners** and ate with them (Mark 2:13–17). Amazing! *He* can do that. But I am warning you: Don't you try this so quickly. Just because Jesus can do it, don't automatically think that you, in your own strength, can emulate him. Take great care that as you reach out to others you do so in the Spirit, with the power that really overcomes sin. Jesus succeeded because people were freed of their sin. When he accepted an invitation from tax collectors, from the morally suspect, he was their friend. They, in turn, gave up their evil ways. Before they knew it, Jesus was leading them to a new way.

Few of us, however, are that advanced. Who can honestly say, "God's spirit fills us! We have some-thing of God which people are seeking!" We must be truly like Jesus before we carelessly and zealously start mingling with the crowd, thinking we can share a drink with them and then lead them to a new life in Christ. Take great care. Jesus must always be honored. There is something so undeniably childlike in him, something so infinitely good. He didn't think about it – the Spirit simply led him and enabled him to see right into the depths of people's hearts. "Here's some-thing that belongs to my Father, to God whom I serve, to whom I sacrifice everything."

Jesus ate with those on the margins of society, yes, but always remember what happened as a result. The people listened to him. They came to him. They

changed. Jesus won them over. He did not preach,
"Change your ways!" He gave them no orders, he just
talked to them and healed them and they changed.
His power and presence brought forth its fruit. All
the more, we must strive to live as he did.

**Do not speak too early** in public, or you will run into
a dragon. Should you eventually become accepted
enough to point unbelievers to God, God will open
doors at the right time. For now it is important that
you stay above water inwardly until those in your
circle of Christians have recognized their spiritual
poverty; for the kingdom of heaven only comes to the
poor. Do not tolerate any quarrelling about dogma –
it should not be a topic of conversation. Preach the
gospel of the kingdom of God, not that of the church.

**Never take pride** in being included in or honored by
respectable society. As ambassadors of the gospel,
we should feel ashamed of being distinguished or
recognized (Luke 6:26). One day God will have all
the important people of this world stand in a corner,
while the rest of the room in God's kingdom will be
filled with the despised and rejected. Proclaim and

work for this Jesus! You will be much happier in your work for God's kingdom if you do.

Wherever Jesus enters into a situation the renewal of society begins – from the bottom up (Luke 4:18–19). Jesus begins with the common people who are so easily overlooked by those in power. It is with them that Jesus begins his work of renewal. He is first and foremost with the downtrodden. He did not say, "I was rich, and you respected me," but, "I was poor, I was hungry, I was thirsty, I was a prisoner, and you came to me" (Matt. 25:35–36). Therefore, concentrate your efforts among the oppressed. From the margins of society comes the power that overcomes the world.

People, including Christians, are afraid of the kind of revolution Jesus brings. But as a worker in God's vineyard you must be looking forward to it. Oh how I wish it would begin today and break to pieces all that causes human misery. Those in power cannot bring about true renewal. The educated and successful people of this world, the good and upright people with all their know-how and piety, try as they may, simply can't do it. Yes, social reformers generate hope and are laudable, but after a short time everything is as bad as before, and sometimes even worse. Many try to do some good, to help the unfortunate not go under. But underneath these various efforts one can see how suppressed people remain. The good culture we have created ends up oppressing and killing thousands of others in the process. Our modern level of prosperity ultimately depends on human sacrifice, on millions having to pay for the privileges we enjoy with all our progress.

Whenever I travel on a train or use some other modern convenience I do so knowing that countless others have slaved away to make this happen. The advantages you and I enjoy mean that thousands suffer. It is at their expense that we live well. How hard we Christians make it for Jesus to fully reign in our midst! Who truly believes in him? Who really lives for the justice of his kingdom? Who genuinely cares about the people and their plight? We cannot just believe in or confess Jesus. As strange as it may sound, we must "believe" in the downtrodden. Believe in the lost, believe in the oppressed, believe in all those who cannot humanly flourish: that is Jesus!

**Jesus chose his disciples** from among the simple people, not because he wants weaklings but because he recognizes strength and durability in those who are downtrodden (James 2:5). They are not weak; they are oppressed, but not feeble. Here, where they work themselves to the bone, straining and striving to wrest a living from the earth around them, every step of their lives won at the cost of sweat and tears, is where Jesus sees the strength that he can use. Here, the highest becomes one with the lowest.

**We should protest** against the peace which tolerates everything as it is (Ezek. 13:10). This includes those religions and teachings that emphasize resignation, as though we should accept and submit to everything because it is somehow God's will. In Jesus there is no such thing as mere resignation. No, in his name we are called to seek God's justice on earth. In Jesus we are to pursue his reign – not just for ourselves but for all people. Those who gather around Jesus cry out for God's kingdom and his justice.

Consider the widow in Jesus' parable (Luke 18:1–8). She cried out with all her strength and determination and did not become weary. She and the people had to have justice; they had the right to live happily in God's world. It is significant that in this parable Jesus identifies God with the unjust world – the widow faces an unjust judge. Words can hardly express the Savior's love when he says: "God is in this unjust world – seek him out." In this world, it seems as if everyone is out for themselves, including those in positions of authority. It is as if God allows everything to go to ruin. So many millions are deprived of their rights and cry out, "Is there no justice, no God in heaven? Doesn't he care what happens to us? Will things ever change?"

The widow runs to the unjust judge and begs again and again: "You must help me!" Today, too, there are millions who cry out, "Oh God, help us!" And in this parable the judge turns around. It is through this human judge that God's will is done. Yes, God has placed us in this unjust world, among worldly authorities, so that we might be used to turn them around, so that God's righteousness will prevail for those who are oppressed and denied what is rightfully theirs.

Look for God's justice. Right where you are, among the people, where it is extremely difficult, where people suffer blows and hard knocks and where you have to fight and wrestle, seek his justice. Right where it looks impossible to change anything, where people desperately fight for their rights and hardly ever think of God, where there is no love or mercy or even consciousness of right and wrong, is where there is the greatest need for God's righteousness to prevail. Right there is where you must work for God and his kingdom.

Part of your task, therefore, is to cry out for justice on behalf of those who for whatever reason can no longer cry out (Prov. 31:8–9). But always do so in the love of God. To seek God's kingdom as Christ showed us cannot be done without love. This is what we learn from Jesus himself, who, moved by compassion, forgave his accusers and tormentors (Luke 23:34). It's not enough to complain about the state of the world or consign it to hell. Keep struggling, fighting, and seeking for God's justice, for it is God who ultimately rules the earth. Indeed, God is waiting to use us as his vessels for his cause. Our struggle is not in vain. So be steadfast. Soft and flabby Christianity will never bring about change in the world.

When you hear people cry out, "We want justice!" listen to them. Indeed, they will have justice. Assure them of this. But show that they must learn to give up their lives for the needs of others for true justice to come. God's justice demands what is right and good for all people. Plead for those who despair, plead daily before the throne of God for justice for all people. Wherever there is injustice, work to push it away, so that people can breathe in God's justice and have hope for God's righteousness. Never tire of praying for this.

**The working class,** or what in the Bible is called the "multitude" (Luke 23:27), has heart. Take note of this. Be sure to have fellowship with the people (2 Cor. 6:11). Listen to them. Hear them out. You will surely experience something quite different than you would by being in a gathering of preachers or in some committee meeting of mission planners. I for one would much rather rub shoulders with ordinary folk where real life pulsates. They say what they think, sometimes crudely, but that does not matter. In Jesus' day, it was those who wept publicly before the Savior – those who were natural and genuine – who experienced God's victory in their midst (Luke 7:36–50).

Whatever you do, don't hide behind the institutional workings of the church or some Christian organization. If you do, those with warm and fervent hearts will hold their tongues and nothing worthwhile will ever come about. Instead, sit with the people who toil every day for their livelihood. Get to know them, chat with them, and reach out with warmth of heart. It will be among these people that you will find a longing for the kingdom of God.

Don't be surprised if you hear some plain speaking, especially regarding preachers and all their churches. Those of us who are considered ministers have no idea how little we are loved. Climb down to where you can hear the groaning of the people. When you see for yourself those who sigh, those who wail and lament, then you will be on the right ground. Only then will you be able to truly work and serve, since these are mostly people who grieve for salvation. Whether they realize it or not, they mourn because the Savior is being crucified on earth. Respect them and you will surely experience something of God.

**People from humble circumstances** are sometimes our angels. The despised of this earth are actually here to help us. Those who usually don't have much to say can sometimes speak the most important word. I have

personally experienced this. Several times God has
sent my way a very humble, rejected person, who said
something unawares which I needed to hear. When
this happens my first reaction is usually, "Why should
*he* have something to say to me?" But then later on
I realize that I am ignoring the very voice of God.
Often God puts someone in our path to prevent an
accident, or to sharpen our character. We must always
be ready to listen and welcome those of humble
circumstances.

# 5

# Open Wide Your Heart

**When you meet people** of other faiths don't hopelessly think to yourself that they are damned. Even when you see people who are involved in wrong dealings, in behaviors you want nothing to do with, don't condemn them. Be careful! Watch out that you don't destroy what heaven has in store. Your neighbors, no matter how pagan they may appear to be, can change, but you must show that you trust them. Yes, if you really believe that they belong to God, then Jesus can overcome any darkness, fill any heart with joy, and turn any person to the Father in heaven (Rom. 5:6–11). Always trust that those you meet belong to God; they will come to him one day. The Savior wants to help all people (2 Pet. 3:9). If God can change you, then when others see what your life is like they will also change. When God's power is seen working in us, it will have an effect far beyond our immediate spheres of influence. In this way, the whole world will receive the Savior's help.

**Jesus lives** in *our* world, the one we can see and feel and grasp with our thoughts and understanding. He is no escapist. Neither is he about to snatch a chosen few and separate them from godless humanity. No, Jesus would rather let himself be called a sinner among sinners, a prostitute and wrongdoer, a glutton and a drunk, than to set himself apart from human misery (Matt. 11:19). When we read, "He is the first-born from among the dead" (Col. 1:18), it means that Jesus appeals to the dead. Tell those who feel as if dead that Jesus is theirs. To those who feel worthless, whose life seems of no value, say: "Your life must be worth something, since Jesus has come into it. Yes, from out of the world of the dead, new life can be born in you."

**If you read the parable** of the treasure buried in the field (Matt. 13:44), it will make you want to pray, "Dear Father in heaven, help us find the hidden treasures of the kingdom of heaven." If you search and dig in the field of life, you will find hidden treasure.

Even in our day, even where everything appears to be confused, where everything is bent on distressing and oppressing us, where everything looks bad – even here, suddenly you can encounter the reign of God. Even in our afflictions, in our anxieties, needs, and struggles, God is there (Ps. 34:18). There is a treasure in them. Therefore sell everything you have and buy the treasure. Cast all your troubles and woes aside, and seek God in whatever situation you are in.

This is how the Savior lived on earth. He did not recoil from the world – not even the wicked world, not even his enemies. He found God the Father even in what was bad: "Thank God! The Almighty is in the world. Now I know why my Father sent me into the world – it contains a treasure!" Jesus goes to a wedding and finds treasure there. He goes into the wilderness and is surrounded by hungry people, and he finds treasure there. He experiences anxiety and finds treasure. He is hung on a cross and groans with pain, he descends into the grave and into hell, and he finds treasure. Father, Father, Father in everything!

Can you and I do likewise? Yes, that is what we must pray for: "Let us find you, God, in all things." Don't lose heart. Whether you are hungry or satisfied, crying or laughing, you have treasure right where you are, and because of that you can forget everything else. Where is our heavenly Father? He is in the world, in the distress, in the anxiety and need, in all our troubles. Have no fear, the treasure remains, for every soul belongs to our loving Father in heaven.

**Fallen human beings** lie in the dirt – yet they are precious stones. A diamond that lies in the dirt cannot glitter. But because it is a jewel, it cannot be spoiled by the dirt. It can be picked up and polished again and sparkle as before. Therefore, when you encounter those who are lying in the dirt, don't think that they are rotten. It is a crime against God's love to think of anybody as being lost or bad. What God has created is never bad. But people can find themselves in the wrong place, and because of this, can give a completely wrong impression. If a jewel is to sparkle, it must be brought into the light somewhere. That is why you should not just tell the unbeliever that he is a sinner. No, first tell him, "God loves you!" Sin gains a stronghold only when we no longer remain faithful to God. It is a sin if the jewel, having once been cleaned, throws itself back into the dirt. But if a person knows nothing of God we should not speak of sin, but of misfortune.

**We are never permitted** to trash anyone, least of all ourselves. No person is evil at the core; they are merely entangled in evil (Rom. 7:7–25). As soon as they have recognized their unworthiness, then the nobler part of themselves that God originally created will be reborn. Consider the centurion from Capernaum who said to Jesus, "I do not deserve to have you come under my roof" (Matt. 8:5–13). But then he added, "But just say the word. . . . " Similarly, when people you meet realize that in spite of sin and guilt God is for them, they will feel called to live for others – yes, the whole need of the world can be laid on their hearts.

**In all that happens,** good or bad, Christ is present. So instead of resignation and worry, we should always trust that things will change, even if we have to go through hell first. For the purpose of life is Christ. God has promised to re-create heaven and earth and bring the whole world into the light of the Savior. "I am making everything new!" (Rev. 21:1–5). This is our hearts' deepest longing, that Christ reconciles the whole cosmos. He is the ruler over all, and his light will fill the entire universe.

Therefore, avoid dividing the world into "us" and "them." If you do, you will harden your heart. There are not two worlds, one in God's hands and the other one not. There are not two species of people either, one totally under God's rule and the other completely outside of it. No devil can do what he wants, no wicked power or principality can act on its own. Even the Evil One is in darkness because of God's will. There he lives his own kind of life, one that is contagious and deadly to those who are attracted by it, yet the entire realm of sin and death remains in God's domain, firmly held in his hands (1 Pet. 3:18–19). Carry this knowledge in your heart as a witness to the lordship of Christ. Boldly proclaim to every devilish spirit, to every demonic stronghold, "You are under God. You cannot make a single move without God. We are all under God!"

Unless you grasp this, you will never experience why Christ came into the world. Even if you should meet someone who is a devil, ultimately he is in God's hands. No other power, no ruler, no one in heaven or on the earth or in hell can move a finger without God's love. "Christ is head over every power and authority" (Col. 2:10). He is Lord over everything. Even if you face a torrent of unbelief and rebellion against God, as powerful as that current might be it is in God's sovereign hands. For Christ's victory has been won. "It is finished" (John 19:30).

Therefore, never fear the devil, for there is no master greater than Jesus. Not even in the deepest depths or blackest night can one escape from yielding to him. There is but one Lord, one God, one Father of all, "who is over all and through all and in all" (Eph. 4:6). No hell, death, or devil can make any such claim. All things are God's because Christ is all in all (Col. 3:11).

If you should have to suffer for him because of your service to the gospel, remember you will also rule with him. Live in this expectation, because God holds everything in his hands. There is but one dominion, and it is God's (1 Cor. 15:20–28). And though there are many who are bound by sin, there is nevertheless one kingdom. There may be two rooms in a house, but it is one house, not two. All things are under God's command. And in the house of God, you may rule with Christ even amid darkness, sin, and death. You need not weaken, nor lose confidence to carry on. You can always go forward.

Let this live in your heart. Don't allow a speck of space in your heart for grumbling about how bad the world is. If you start to grumble, you will lose sight of the victory of God. Whatever you do, don't ever condemn the godless or unbelievers (1 Cor. 5:9–11). That is not your business. In fact, don't even think of people as unbelieving – they are not unbelieving, only tormented. They cannot open their own eyes, they are drunk with their misery, saturated with distress, and can't see the stars for the roof. All the more you must witness to the truth that God is God and there is no other, and that he offers hope to everyone.

This does not mean that sin and evil will not be judged (2 Thess. 1:5–10). But the hour of judgment is God's concern alone. Until that time, your duty is to make known the name of Jesus to any and every person. Believe in Jesus' victory, holding out the possibility of redemption to everyone (1 John 2:1–2). Whoever comes to you, wherever you may be, proclaim: "You will be saved, for you belong to Jesus. God's will is that no one, including you, be lost, but that everyone repent and live." Not everyone will grasp this, nor is it necessary. People don't have to be "converted" to our Christianity. But in the long run, millions must be transferred to the rule of God, to the lordship of Christ. They *must* go in even though they yell and howl. Haven't we all at one time or another kicked and screamed?

If you or I should have to give up hope for any person, any country, any domain, or any situation, then Jesus is not the one who holds the universe together. There would still remain the burden of death, of travail, a load of night and darkness. Then Jesus is not the light of the world. His is not a cosmic cross that brings everything back together (Col. 1:15–20). He is not, finally, victorious. For what else can Jesus' resurrection mean but eternal hope for all he holds together? Believe, therefore, that all that opposes God must come to an end, that hell, death, and sin must cease (Rev. 21:1–4). Believe that every realm belongs to God, and be determined to spread the love of God wherever you are. If you fail to do this, you will not be able to freely rejoice in your faith and calling, nor confidently invite sinners to believe the gospel themselves.

I know from personal experience of people who have been set free simply by my reminding them, "You belong with me, because you and I belong to God."

"Oh, no," they say. "I am a terrible person."

"No matter," I reply. "You belong with me."

"But you do not know the evil things I have done," they say.

"Nevertheless," I tell them, "you belong with me, and I belong with you, for both of us belong to God." It's amazing how this truth changes people. They receive so much encouragement just by this exchange that there is simply no more talk of wickedness or sinfulness.

Once there was a kleptomaniac who came to me seeking to be healed, who continued in this way for a long time, also after we got to know each other. In spite of this, I kept telling him, "You and I belong together. No matter how long you go on stealing, I will not let you go." Lo and behold, after a time he gave up stealing and become a totally different person. How many others – proud, avaricious, jealous, or quarrelsome people – have been given power to change simply because they felt, for the first time, genuine human solidarity. How much happens when people finally realize that they belong to Jesus. I mean truly realize, not with trite religious words. When people become conscious that they belong to Christ, sin melts away.

Always think in cosmic terms. The gospel of hell, the gospel of Satan, the gospel of lies must be trodden down, so that at last Jesus, the Living One, can redeem *all* creation. The kingdom of this world will become the kingdom of our Christ (Rev. 11:15). Evil will capitulate before the name of Jesus. The powers of death and destruction will submit and be redeemed. Yes, demons too, whatever they may be – deceit, sickness, death, corruption, misery – are captives. They too are in misery. Therefore, Christ's victory must be for them as well (Eph. 4:8). Pray for this. Christ's redemption will dissolve the darkness, and the light of God's glory will one day fill creation, so much so that every tongue in heaven and on earth and under the earth will confess that Jesus Christ is Lord (Phil. 2:10–11). This power, which makes holy those who are evil and redeems those who are lost, will finally overcome all inhuman forces, all spirits that mock God, right down into the depths of hell. The victory is ours. God *will* be all in all.

**God's love tears down walls** (Eph. 2:14). No longer religion against religion, Christians against non-Christians, but justice against sin, life against death. Therefore, every person you encounter should be your concern. Do not settle for less. The whole world must see the glory of God. I hope you become free to share in the gifts God gives to those you live amongst. This is our hope, but its fulfillment will have to be fought for.

God protects the oppressed. He will see to it that they receive his blessing. Today his Spirit moves upright hearts everywhere, without asking what religion they cling to. Our task is to spread the gospel of Christ, not the gospel of Christians. Christ does not want separation. This is difficult for us to keep in mind. It is not easy to interact with those whose lives are sinful without yielding to the pressure of either compromising or distancing oneself. I hope, however, that we will experience the all-embracing, creative power of Christ.

This is why we need to stand on the side of the humble, the working class – those who eke out an existence in this world and live accordingly. Tragically, the church has abandoned them to darkness. Yet this same church lives with this darkness, and in so doing absorbs the very same sinful principles that rule the world. Our calling as Christ's ambassadors is to serve, not rule. The chief thing is to be an apostle of Jesus Christ, not an apostle of the Christian world or religion. Have patience, and whatever you do, steer clear of forming a sect or party. Your work must embrace the whole spectrum of society, and your integrity must win you everyone's trust.

**Have you ever looked** at the world to see what is driving it, what it has dreamed up in the way of worshipping God in some way? The whole creation is thirsting for God. Human history is but a burning thirst for God. "What do I care about God!" people say, and yet they go on to create their own gods anyway. And then they cry out for God's mercy as soon as life overwhelms them.

Whether people are pagan, Muslim, or Christian, or find it impossible to believe, Jesus hears their cries.

So suffer with those you meet, and love them. All the misery of this world stems from a deep thirst which results from living far away from God. The heavy load of sin that presses down on people with such satanic power leads millions into wrong and perverse ways, into dark paths of idolatry and sin, confusion and twisted thoughts about God. All the more, keep your heart open to hear their heartache.

**In every person** there exists a thirst for life, a desire to rise in the world, and not just in those who find themselves at the very bottom of human existence. When misguided, this thirst can lead to great barbarity and cruelty. Most people try to quench this thirst with material things, with pleasures that only generate further temptation and delusion. They are under the illusion that if they only possessed this or that or could achieve this or that, their sense of lack would be met. As a result, they are left with nothing but disappointment (1 John 2:15–17). Even after striving for every possible freedom and convenience, greed for more floods into their hearts and they collapse inwardly. In gaining the whole world, they still have gained nothing (Mark 8:36).

The problem is that people confuse their human thirst with that which comes from God. Instead of satisfying our godly thirst, of the soul, we immerse ourselves in material things, fruitlessly trying to satiate the desires of the flesh. But Jesus swept this all aside. He did not tackle material poverty head-on by introducing a program of social reforms. Instead, he showed people that their thirst for the things of this world is not the same as a godly thirst. He understood well their longing for a better existence, for a better world, but he showed them how important it is not to get swept away into the whirlpool of human desire. He pointed the people to something higher, to a real thirst in which our deepest desires and needs are fulfilled.

Jesus saw straight into people's lives, right into their inner thirsting (John 4:1–14). He was moved to compassion by how lost they had become in the superficialities of existence – crushed, sighing, mired in rebellion. And because he saw their plight with eyes of mercy, they responded (Matt. 9:35–38). By the quiet light of his presence he helped them to realize that they were destined for a more abundant life. He ignited in them a deeper, divine burning that would fulfill their heart's desire, a fervent wish for something brand new, something from above, that could be experienced here and now and lead them to becoming true persons.

So don't be surprised or alarmed that the thirst in those you meet is misguided. Such thirst is not quickly quenched. But don't despair. The water that springs not from this world but from God can and will quench our thirst. What people actually thirst for is something better than what this temporal world can offer. All the more you must always seek to turn people to the one who alone can quench their thirst. "Come to me, all you who are weary and burdened, and I will give you rest" (Matt. 11:28). The living Christ alone is the source that can satisfy our souls. From him flow streams of living water. From whom else come mercy, love, forbearance, forgiveness – all those things we all deeply thirst for?

**In Jesus' day,** the tax collectors and sinners, the worldly – the unbelievers, as they became known later – had a deep hunger for God (Luke 18:9–14). This is why as soon as Jesus came onto the scene it was the despised who came running to him. Their hearts were already open and so they responded, "Yes, that applies to me. Is that God speaking to me? Yes, it *is* God! If that's what he says, I believe!" That's why they came; the outcasts, the ones who had no use for pious restrictions, who lived their lives not according to some law but as they themselves thought best. All of a sudden, as often happens when something is revealed by God, a great longing arose within them and like a magnet they were drawn to the Savior. Nothing reveals the greatness of Jesus as much as this – he sat down and ate with sinners. Who is doing this today?

**Every person will be judged** on the basis of whether his heart has been turned toward his fellow human beings or not. He will not be asked, "What did you believe, and what did you not believe?" All who show compassion can be of service in God's kingdom. Only those who are inhuman cannot be used by God. A person with heart may not yet understand Jesus, but this doesn't mean he despises Jesus or can't be used by God (Mark 9:39–41). Many unbelievers will enter the kingdom of heaven simply because their hearts respond to the needs of others (Matt. 21:31).

**To be a servant of God,** your spirit must be noble and unfettered. You will need to have a very large vision of God's kingdom, one in which everyone and every living thing belongs. Division, disunity, and judgment have harmed God's cause again and again. If you want to serve Jesus, who is King of kings and Lord of lords, you must understand that the world belongs to God, and that God does not want to relinquish any part of it. You must see that Christ lays claim on everyone – whether high or low, good or bad. Everything that lives belongs to God. And this truth should be not only in our heads but in our blood and in every breath. As a servant of Jesus Christ, do not give up on anyone – even the worst sinner. We have to believe, for ourselves and for others, that we all belong to God. I may be stupid and clumsy – I may even commit grave sin – but my true self, which is created in God's image, belongs to God. Neither sin nor death can change this fact.

# 6

# Make God's Love Known

**How it must pain our Savior** to see his people place a
limit on God's love! Faith trusts that God loves the
world. He loves the worst of sinners. Oh, how many
"believing" people have been drawn away from this
faith!

Give yourself completely to this one fact: God
loves the world. Don't let anything interfere with
this truth. Even when you can't quite grasp it, believe
in God's love, which is for all people. The Bible
condemns anything that undermines the faith that
seeks to bless everyone. In Christ there is a ray of
hope for every single person. Though thousands
are outside the realm of faith, nonetheless they can
still come in. So don't judge others; judge yourself
instead for your own disbelief (James 2:12–13). Your
lack of faith in God's great power to save the world,
your small-mindedness, which cannot imagine a God

capable of a world-encompassing love, does more harm to the gospel than those who profess no faith. Be on guard, therefore, against such disbelief. Otherwise it will be you who hears, "I don't know you or where you come from. Away from me, all you evildoers!" (Luke 13:27)

**Jesus loves us in advance,** before we are ever worthy of his love (1 John 4:19). He loves us before God's kingdom has fully come. He loves us while we are sinners, because his love comes from eternity. But just because of that, his love is combined with judgment. His love is not soft. It does not overlook our sin. That is not love. Jesus' love hangs on the cross and works to purify us. Jesus' love is our salvation from sin. This is the gospel: "You are loved!"

Therefore, love each person with Christ's love. That is not easy. You will meet people who look evil and repulsive. They won't want to be loved; they would rather look after themselves. All the more, love them in the spirit of Jesus. Let no partition separate "them" from "us." There is hope for all. Hate the evil, but not the people who do evil. With the Savior, look past the ugly exterior of people's lives and into their hearts.

Have you ever looked into someone's *heart* and found it to be unworthy of love?

Christ's love can convert people and conquer whole nations and societies without them even noticing it. Your vocation as a follower of Christ is to regard *everyone* as a future citizen of God's kingdom. Therefore, bring them into God's kingdom by loving them as Jesus does. Only then will the chains fall that still bind them. God's kingdom will envelop all people before they know it, and this will certainly change their lives. They will gradually be given different hearts and new thoughts. Then the time will come when their deepest needs will be met.

**The love of God** melts away everything that is bad, everything that is sordid, everything that leads to despair. It banishes the night and vanquishes death. But this love is not human love as we understand it. It loves enemies and rejects no one. God's love strides unswerving through everything, like a hero, and will not be insulted, despised, or rejected; it marches through the world with the helmet of hope on its head.

Don't hold back, therefore, but be bold in proclaiming this love – that all created beings are loved. Don't lose courage because you see so many people who seem to follow only their selfish desires – as if they enjoyed the sinful life. Don't be fooled. No one is happy being a sinner. Everyone groans under the weight of their sin. But God's love goes boldly among all who are groaning in death. Jesus wants all people to know that he himself is the boundless love of God. He is the flame by which we can be purified to live a life of love.

**Most people** who get all worked up about injustice are motivated by a sense of rage, and that is their mistake. The purer the gospel is, the more ferment or turmoil there will be. The mistake is to think that turmoil must arise from resentment and be sustained by anger. The breakthrough that comes from God is based on love.

There have been too many movements and revolutions born of hatred; the transformation of earth and heaven and humankind, as God has planned them to be, has too often been co-opted by human frustration. Ferment and change indeed come with Jesus. But Christ represents God's love, and he wants to pour the love of God into every human heart. His love condemns no one (Rom. 8:34–35). It raises the lowly from the dust – all the poor, rejected, despised, and suffering shall see help coming. So be careful as you rebel or work against the present state of affairs. Seek God's justice, but do so through love. Jesus needs a people who, in the power of the Spirit, will transform everything out of love. All things in heaven and on earth must become new through love.

If you find it difficult to believe in God's new creation, then love those whom you can love. Just give your love to everyone you meet. Most people are unable to express themselves about formal faith or deep spiritual matters, but everyone understands what love is. Let love surge up in your heart and you will be one with God's great mission on earth. If you want to find your way forward, if you want to represent the kingdom of God in anticipation of a new heaven and a new earth, then commit yourself first and foremost to love. "God so loved the world . . ." (John 3:16–18). Any sincere follower of Christ can see that; how else can one ever believe that God makes everything new? See what is good in the world, love, and do not let yourself be bound up by anger, no matter how righteous the cause.

**If you want to be** true evangelists of the gospel to those who are bound by sin, then the gospel must be, as with Paul, a power from God, not a speech or a command (Rom. 1:16). The gospel is a power, not merely a message. Therefore you must keep it pure. To combine the gospel with threats or pressure makes it unclean; light and darkness get mixed.

This is why it is so important that you keep telling those you meet, "You belong to God." God defends the rights of humanity. God is love and cannot abide the thought of a single person not belonging to him. Right now millions of people live in darkness, but they will all be freed. That is why we, too, must defend this right for every person. To condemn anyone upholds the power of sin and death. As soon as you or I or anyone else writes someone off, God is denied a certain right. You must instead commit each soul to God's care and keep that soul in mind as one for whom God's right will also come to light. Otherwise, you are not a faithful witness of Jesus. And you must believe the same for yourself. That is the gospel.

**Just as the Savior** had his cross to carry, so must we. The fact that we have a cross is actually proof that we are near him. "Whoever does not carry their cross and follow me cannot be my disciple" (Luke 14:27). So begins our participation in the need of the world. This participation goes deep and will bring you into collision with the world. As a witness to Christ, your cross is to endure whatever the world throws at you. You may be determined to embrace the world with God's love, but don't be surprised when it pushes you away – partly out of stupidity, partly through misunderstanding, and partly due to despair.

When such a cross falls on you, be careful not to let yourself grow bitter or cynical. The Savior never responded to his enemies with bitterness (1 Pet. 2:23). He sees the ignorance of people and forgives them. The cross of Jesus bears good fruit because it remains in God's love. And wherever there exists something of God's love, Christ's redemptive work is present. So take up your cross, but remember that love must be present. It has to be your priority. If you will not love, then stay away from Christ's cause. If you get insulted and can't forget it, then stay away from Christ's cross.

Seek to be someone from whom God's love radiates. That love is the strongest power in the world. Without it, your faith and zeal will not achieve much in God's kingdom. Love alone judges perfectly, builds soundly, and always redeems.

**The gospel of Christ** is eternally new. "Sing to the Lord a new song!" (Isaiah 42:10) Jesus comes to us as a man, and we must represent him as such. His work in us can only begin when we are one with him. So *be* a "savior," a helper to the people in all simplicity. Let love be the guiding force that brings you together with others, conscious that "I no longer live, but Christ lives in me" (Gal. 2:20). Too often, those who call themselves Christians respect only fellow Christians. They want to make people like them before accepting them into their company. Jesus, however, is the sinner's companion, and leaves everything else up to his Father in heaven.

You stand before God, and between you and God lies the world. Through your faith, allow God to work in the midst of all the confusion that exists around you. You yourself cannot wade in and do anything, but if you stand rightly among the lost sheep who have no shepherd, God's spirit will make headway. When Jesus speaks of workers in the harvest (Matt. 9:37–38) he does not mean missionaries, but powers of God – angels, the Holy Spirit, or however else one wants to put it. The apostles only received and passed on the sheaves in service to God.

This is how you should see your vocation. The unbelieving whose hearts God has readied will come to you. Receive them with patience and love. They will still be a long way from recognizing the truth, since this only comes after they feel accepted. But they will feel accepted when, in God's love, you count them as belonging to God even before they have recognized him and just because they came to you.

**If we are messengers for God,** then we have the authority to proclaim salvation, preach peace, and speak about forgiveness to all people – the great and the humble, the rich and the poor, the just and the depraved. We therefore no longer concentrate on misery, perversity, or godlessness. The whole world laments these already. Individuals already weep over their own imperfection and sin, over the impossibility of ever doing any real good. You and I must remember that the crucified Jesus strides into this misery, under which people suffer terribly, and proclaims the good news: Your sins have been forgiven. Be comforted. The godlessness and wick-edness that is all around you, and which has also taken root in you and embittered your life, will not be triumphant. It will be wiped out – forgiven. You belong to God, to your Father in heaven. Salvation is coming!"

So proclaim the triumph of goodness – proclaim God's salvation. And when you do, believe that people can once again do what is right and good. People need to sense that we trust them, that they are God's children, and that deep down they have a feeling for what is right. Trust the people and preach the good news; then you will find the way to their hearts. Wherever you go, believe that people can become good, in the name of the Savior.

# 7

# Show the Gospel

**Just because** you are a representative of the gospel doesn't give you the right to shout, "I have the truth to proclaim to you!" There are far too many preachers who rely only on human insights and operate on a human level. It's not surprising that there is hardly an echo from unbelievers. Though this may be because it is simply not the right moment, perhaps it's because we are not worthy – we don't possess the inner light to call others. If we hope to save the lost, this light first has to be clearly visible where God's rulership is already accepted. Otherwise, who are we to go and preach?

The day of God must shine among us if non-Christians are ever going to respond. How can we point others to the great day of redemption unless the clear light of the Son of Man streams through us (1 Cor. 4:17)? Only when you experience something of God yourself will you have the confidence to believe that your neighbor can have what you have. Only then will you be able, when you meet the most blatant sinners, to hold your hand over them in the name of the One who has given you light and say to them, "Since the light has come into my life, it must also come down to you."

**A missionary** should live and bring life in the name of Jesus, not religious strife or debate. True religion is built up on a living people whom God has made alive, not the other way round. Overly religious Christians with all their piety cannot bring the life that God wants. I pray that you may live in Christ, have him in your heart, and convey him to everyone, even in your so-called worldly contacts with people. The Holy Spirit who leads us has nothing to do with party politics or violence; at all levels of society this Spirit changes people, and they give themselves to what is good and true. This Spirit works in the world for the sake of the world, without forming groups which divide the world between "us" and "them."

We don't need more preachers but more, much more, of the Spirit (1 Thess. 1:5). The spirit of God must come to meet you from out of the people them-selves, and this will happen, for it is the way God works today. Think of yourself as a watchman; every true witness of Christ is one of God's watchmen on the walls of the city to which all people shall come (Mic. 4:2). Then there will be a true situation from God – not a Western or European influence but a divine work. Do what comes to your hands. Rejoice when your helplessness hinders you from becoming a slave to human principles and human counsel, and be joyful in spirit.

**Believe me:** Truth never wins with words alone (1 Cor. 4:20). God's truth is not revealed in beautiful talks or ideas. It manifests itself when God's greatness and goodness are seen, especially in those who confess his name. Those who meet you will feel this. They will also sense that you respect them, even when you have to confront their wrongdoing. Because of how you are, deep down they will be grateful when they have to face what they have done wrong.

But as soon as you think of yourself as the moral and righteous one and others as immoral and unrigh-teous, then you ruin what God wants to do. The power of the Spirit will flee. Never despise other people, no matter who they are or how far they have strayed. Have and show a deep respect for everyone you meet. How can others find the love of God, who is the Father of all and who is love, if we his representatives look down on them?

Remember, Jesus went directly to those who were outcasts. He much preferred to associate with the "sinners" than with those who proudly set themselves apart. Jesus shared the lot of the downtrodden because God himself loves those rejected by society, those the world deems unworthy. God wants to help *all* people, and raise the dignity they possess to the light.

**Religious clichés** will get you nowhere. There must be tangible results of what Christ can do (Acts 8:4–8). Therefore, seek to show kindness and pay attention to all who come your way, even those who oppose what you represent. Showing concern in outward things is often the first step, and sometimes the only step, in proclaiming the love of God to people. It may mean self-denial on your part, but such sacrifice is pleasing to God. What better thing can we do than to please God? It may be that you can only help in a practical way, yet it will count; it can help to further God's kingdom.

Your deeds are of greater significance than you might imagine. For in each gift there is some kind of sacrifice; something of God is in it. The most rewarding thing is doing some deed, especially in humdrum daily life, which makes God glad. You may have much to give or perhaps only a little, but if you give yourself as fully as you know how, even if the deed is quite unassuming, then something can happen to help hasten God's coming kingdom.

**Your witness** is less a matter of influencing people in a religious way than seeking to give them an example by your life (Phil. 1:27). People will take notice of this more and more. By producing good fruit in your own life, you will lead your neighbors and friends to overcome their problems (1 Tim. 4:15–16). From you they will learn to overcome themselves. Jesus wants to give life – genuine life under God, shaping earthly conditions in love and truth. The world needs people of life, not pious hypocrites. Satan will be overcome by authentic living, not by a lot of words.

**I find that the kind** of evangelizing which pushes people into a religious experience leads to great disappointments. We must advance the gospel only through our presence, which should be as simple and clear as possible, containing a life hidden in Christ. Then we have to wait until God opens hearts. What we try to instill or bring about inevitably falls to pieces. Aiming for greater numbers also has little effect. Do your duty as best as you are able – don't overdo it – and you will be inwardly strong before God, without attempting to achieve something greater than what God wants. It is discouraging to see how unreceptive the world seems regarding deeper truths. So it is a great compensation when now and then we experience the opening of a heart. The time must first be ripe.

**We are faced** with a paradox: the gospel of God's kingdom awaits future fulfillment, yet it must be lived out, here and now. We must be able to offer people something they can find nowhere else, and it must be something of real practical value. If people had to rely on what pastors typically do for them, we would be in a bad way. We can't live from sermons. What people care about are actual improvements. In other words, what people want and need is a practical faith. Be on guard against separating religion and life!

**In your work** you will be surrounded by people who rarely think or wonder about God. They have many other things on their minds. This is why it is so important that you direct yourself toward giving thanks to God. God needs people who know how to give thanks (1 Thess. 5:16–18). To give thanks *is* to give witness. Even one thankful person will bring God honor. When God gives us his blessing and we receive it in thankfulness, he bestows his power upon us, and through that we can live happily among those who don't yet believe. Something good will flow from our lives. The Savior tells us: "The mouth speaks what the heart is full of. A good man brings good things out of the good stored up in him, and an evil man brings evil things out of the evil stored up in him" (Matt. 12: 34–35). When our hearts are filled with the goodness that comes from God, it flows out from our hearts and touches the lives of others. Then God's goodness in the world will surely increase.

**It is good** to concern yourself with the practical problems that affect people's everyday lives. Those who carry the kingdom of God in their hearts must also carry this foundation of love and forbearance for all people into the political sphere, because politics shapes the well-being or distress, the growth or decline, of the people. If the people of God do not accept stewardship of humanity in the humble things that lie at hand, how will they be able to communicate the Spirit that dwells within them?

Striving for the Spirit through Bible knowledge and teaching alone results in fanaticism; the world remains in wickedness. This is why godless people have always taken earthly affairs in hand, leaving the children of truth and love to sigh in their self-made corners about the world – over which they ought to be exercising an influence. Therefore, take up earthly, political matters and, once you have made yourself familiar with the issues, quietly go to those in the government with your concerns, and if you can, with some practical tips from your own experience as well.

I cannot stress enough that God's spirit can only work if we are with the people, as Jesus was when he healed so many. An abstract faith based on theology is impotent (1 Cor. 8:1). We ourselves must be tangible expressions of the love and truth of God, seeking to bring light and life into the outer circumstances of life. But if you want God to prevail in this, it will require far greater divine strength than is apparent today. There are far too many human spirits actively at work, each claiming to give the best advice or the most effective approach.

There is a spirit among today's Christians that has no understanding of God's kingdom, and more and more unbelievers are annoyed by it. This same spirit is probably active where you are, and it is sure to offend people. Pay no attention. Just carry on, and let your deeds speak for you. If Jesus is not a living reality, giving birth to deeds, then he is no greater than any other teacher. But he lives – he is the rock on which we stand, and deeds born of his spirit will become the rocks upon which the sins of the world are shattered (Luke 20:18).

**In every country** we see the same confusion and help-lessness. The masses cry out against oppression, but the government lies like an immovable gravestone over them. Everywhere there is human tyranny, which would rather massacre entire peoples than yield an inch.

The prince of this world is the dominant force behind all government (Eph. 6:12). This is more distressing when governments claim a Christian basis. Jesus and his spirit cannot rule because our human schemes maintain absolute control.

In view of the demonic forces behind the world's government, I do not expect that attempts to influence the government politically will achieve very much. Anyone who wants to save a distressed people will be throttled by the powers that be. Nonetheless, I am not opposed to encouraging enlightened people to go into government work to undertake some sort of resistance. But they must be trustworthy and help people obtain the freedom to organize themselves, at least economically.

Your main task, with God's help, is to train people – in the schools or wherever else you have connections – who represent God's truth and put the well-being of their neighbor above everything else. For this we need the power of God's spirit. We must wait patiently for this power. We can only do what lies in front of us every day, and will often do so with much sighing, for it all seems in vain. Yet I believe that there is progress taking place quietly, and that a new time is being prepared.

**Seek to win hearts.** Jesus is truly proclaimed only when we win hearts for him. True mission does not occur when there is a lot of activity and noise about Jesus. God's Word is alive in stillness, when the Spirit opens hearts to it. His Word is not heard because people are sitting in church, or because they are reading the Bible or are being taught theology, but because their hearts have been opened. This includes those of us who proclaim God's Word (Eph. 1:17–18). We must be among the ones who are being preached to. Even if we have already come to God, remember that this is not because God loves us more than the others, but because he wants to use us as his tools to help others follow him.

Don't consider yourself as blessed and others who don't believe as condemned. Instead, consider everyone you meet who has yet to come to faith to be under God's blessing. Learn to die daily to yourself, for you too, if you are honest, are in some ways a "pagan," even though you can testify that you have heard and believed in the gospel. Beware of the grave danger of becoming arrogant simply because you know something that others don't. It is not knowledge that counts, but becoming a new creature.

**You have probably** already experienced this, but great warmth comes into your heart whenever you are able to forgive sins. There is nothing greater, nothing more blessed, nothing that lifts one's spirits more than this power to forgive sins. It is the power of the gospel.

Certainly without Christ we would not have the courage to meet people (who are often full of darkness) with the authority to forgive sins. But if Jesus stands behind you, you have that authority. Anyone can judge and condemn – the world and the churches do plenty of that! The authority given to you as a minister of the gospel is the strength to forgive without judging and condemning. In this forgiveness resides the power of God's spirit to create new people. When you tell someone that they belong to God, you are telling them that everything about them can change. Even if the impulse to sin is still in them and they find themselves falling back into sin, their life can still come under the power of God's forgiveness.

Who they truly are as God created them to be will come out all right. Once they realize this, they will want to give up their selfishness.

**If you want** to be a true fighter for Jesus, don't be offended when people hate you. Don't feel insulted or strike back (1 Pet. 4:12–19). The whole struggle for God's kingdom consists in laying down your life for others. In this way, even the people who oppose you shall receive life. Rather die than let your love for others be stolen from you. You will certainly make mistakes, like arguing too much with those who disagree with you. But let your aim be to give witness to friendship and goodness, for God is faithful to all people. Hold firmly to the truth that every person, even your worst enemy, belongs to God. Fight with all your strength that more and more people realize this. Believe that God will help each soul to become different. The more faithful you are in this, the more hate against you will be burned away. Hate has a short life. It is love that lives forever.

**We live in an age** in which everything precious is endangered. In spite of all our many "Christian" efforts, all our mission activities, the cities of our world are getting worse, not better. And how much Christian activity there has been in our time, at home and abroad! Never before has the gospel been preached so far and so wide, and yet with so little impact. It is shocking when you see how many Christians gradually retreat, slipping a little here, a little there – people who were once "serious believers," but who have drifted away into a life of respectability. How hideous it is when nothing can be called unbelief anymore! Underneath it all is nothing but an obsession with the comforts of this world. There is so little compulsion for Christ or his cause, and consequently today's Christianity is little more than idle talk. But it cannot go on like this.

We desperately need the simplicity of heart that releases the power of Jesus into this world. The world pants and groans under a thousand woes, and here we are with all our Christianity, without any decisive help. In a war, the time comes when you have to drop the skirmishing and risk your life in order to gain the major objective. Engaging in spiritual battle is no different. Everything else should recede into the background in light of one desire: to descend single-heartedly into the hells of this earth and take over enemy territory. I repeat: into the depths of hell, where endless misery clings to individual hearts and leads to sin and corruption. Here is where you should fight.

God will protect you if you willingly and trustingly descend into the depths of human need. But you must wage war in faith. If you do, Christ will preserve you, even in the midst of the worst things. For it is in the most horrendous events that the victory of Christ is revealed. But, again, you must believe like a child. Avoid anything that gets too complicated. Look only to what Jesus is doing. Don't strive to be clever or sophisticated. And don't overanalyze or try to make everything work out. Only when you are weak are you strong (2 Cor. 12:7–10).

# 8

# Allow the Spirit to Work

**We can accomplish nothing** for God's kingdom on the basis of human strength. All we can say is, "We are unworthy servants; we have only done our duty" (Luke 17:10). Jesus empowers the workers in his vineyard to overcome the world. It is not we who do it, but the Spirit, who acts in and through us and before whom all other spirits must bow. This is what you will experience when hearts turn to you. See to it, then, that God alone works. God is like the sun that sends its rays everywhere, even into the grimiest places.

Whatever you do, don't deliver the work of God into the grasping clutches of religious or political institutions. We can only expect a victory over nominal "Christianity" through the movement of life and yearning in the people. God will give us the hearts of the people, and then our false Christian idols will collapse.

**You may have to wait,** sometimes for years, before you see any improvement. It will be tempting either to compromise and say, in the face of sin and suffering, "We can't really do anything; it's human nature," or to try to force something through in your own strength. Don't let yourself slide into either temptation. Jesus alone can save what is lost, and he will. Certainly you, and any gifts you may have, cannot overcome what drags people down (1 Cor. 3:5–7). Not even your good intentions, which some mistake as faith, can help. Your fight, your struggle, is to let *Christ's* power, not yours, prove itself.

**We must learn to become silent** before God and wait for him. To make a big noise in the name of Jesus has never advanced anything from God. Those who make a big to-do not only ignore the cross but soon run out of steam. Everyone from Noah on has had to learn to become silent. Thousands of people have proclaimed, "I belong to the Lord," but the world has taken no notice. When the Savior said to his disciples, "Go into all the world" (Mark 16:15), his final words were, "I am with you always" (Matt. 28:20), which means, "Take heed, because it is not in your hands. *I* will do it."

So don't blow your own horn! If you want to start a big movement, then go ahead and make a big splash; if you want to be renowned, then go ahead and sound off. But if you want to see God's kingdom advance, stand before the cross and be quiet. God's kingdom will not come into being by our efforts; only God can bring about his reign. We are not expecting an improved society. This is not what we are ultimately working for. God alone has the power to put the stamp of his divinity on human beings and to ennoble what is true and genuine.

In your personal life, too, remain quiet. Guard against exaggeration. And don't chatter about spiritual and religious matters or think about yourself too much either. By becoming too preoccupied with ourselves and what we can do, we end up talking too much and then take our salvation into our own hands. We need people who know they belong to God but who are quietly natural about it. We will never catch a glimpse of what God is doing by strenuous thinking or strategizing – godly matters come unnoticed into hearts ready to receive them. It is God who puts his truth into people's hearts through his Spirit, truth that will flow out of them by itself, like one's breath.

**Try not to busy yourself** too much; instead, humbly let God do the work. Then something will surely come from God. We must always remind ourselves: "Let's hold back! We must not become important; we must not want to force any of our ideas through." Hold back so that the work you do doesn't become your thing (1 Cor. 2:1–5). Jesus is alive, and his victory must be your first concern.

This means you must learn to accept your weakness, your own poverty, and your own limitations, especially when the going gets rough. It is just through your weakness that our Savior can do his work (2 Cor. 12:9). He can manage what you cannot! Therefore, be prudent in pushing your own ideas so that your ego doesn't take over.

It's often better not to get too involved in other peoples' affairs, wanting to have a say in everything, because most of the time we don't really know what the right step is. In the end, only God can work things out. Especially where there is sickness, poverty, or strongholds of temptation, you will have to realize your helplessness. You don't need to be a knight in shining armor who is all set to kill the devil – no, we must learn to step back in faith and hope and keep the power of Jesus firmly in the center. He is at hand, and what we should desire most is that he does *his* miracles and signs. When this happens, we can indeed rejoice.

**If you tell people** to their face about their sins, they will not respond. Their ears and their hearts are already blocked by sin. So don't think you can speak to people's hearts by taking a frontal attack. Part of them may respond, but they will invariably flee. No, there is only one way to speak to people – the way the Savior showed us. He was like a lamb before the shearer. He bore our sins (Isa. 53:7–12). As a follower of Jesus Christ you too, without sparing yourself, must carry sin. In other words, you must learn to be silent and suffer like Christ – you must carry in your heart the sin of this world before God. Then wherever you go and whomever you meet, there will be in you a living witness against sin. You will not have to use many words. People will feel it.

People have to realize their own sin for themselves. This comes through *God's* judgment, not yours. Only then will they come to God. You or I can never make people mourn for their sin. No one can. God alone penetrates into their unconscious, into the invisible domains where everything comes out, both the good and the bad. Seek therefore to draw God into this realm, into those hidden streams of sin that keep people in bondage. By suffering with the people you can bring their need to God and sigh, "When will they open their eyes?" This attitude is the kind of sermon people need to feel. If you speak in this inward way, when you ache for God's truth and live by it, when you cry out for mercy and grace and judgment, so that sins are revealed through the Spirit, then things start to happen.

# 9

# Always Hope

**Never give up on anyone.** No one, and I mean no one, can escape God (Ps. 139). Even if people were to live in the depths of the sea, lost from sight, God would still follow after them. Go where they wish, do what they will, they will end up in God's hand. And that is very fortunate, also for humankind in general. However far astray people happen to go, they still remain in God's hand. Even when they have committed every possible sin and everything about them looks as though they are as far from God as one can get, Christ will lead them back and hold them with his right hand. Light can penetrate any darkness, the blackest night, for help is at hand in every possible situation.

Even to the Pharisees Jesus said, "The kingdom of God is in your midst" (Luke 17:20–21). Why? Because in his love he refuses to let himself be severed from anyone, even his bitterest enemies. He sees them as in bondage, but he also sees in them the seed of God's kingdom. In Jesus, God has planted a seed within every person. This seed must sprout so that God's kingdom comes forth from them – from you and from me, from Jews and Gentiles, from the devout and the godless. This will be the marvel when God's kingdom appears: it will not be the work of anyone great but something living that thrives and grows from millions of people.

**From every pulpit,** and in every street and workplace, it should be proclaimed: "You all belong to God! Whether you are godless or devout, under judgment or under grace, blessed or damned, you belong to God, and God is good and wants what is best for you. Whether you are dead or alive, righteous or unrighteous, in heaven or in hell, you belong to God, and as soon as you are swept into the current of faith, the good within you will emerge." Speak like this and you will have different results from those who peddle the truncated gospel that gives with one hand and takes away with the other.

If only Christian self-righteousness could be driven from our hearts once and for all! If only the passion for judging others would stop! If only we would learn to see sin more like a disease and separate the sinner from the sin! Our faith must be a light from God that draws people into the stream of new life. Then the most godless will become righteous.

God loved us even when we were his enemies. If God loved you when you were still a sinner and drew you into the stream that led you to himself (Rom. 5:6–11), then surely it is only a matter of time before those you try to help will also enter the current of faith. But if you throw obstacles into the stream, if you have certain "Christian" or religious misgivings, how can there ever be a current that sweeps up all the people of this world?

**Why are so many millions** sighing and grieving? Why do they experience so little inner peace in their lives, even when outwardly they appear to be happy and have what they need? People are always looking for something, even though they don't know what it is. In even the most perverse people beat hearts that feel something of the truth. Don't forget this. Yes, in the shadows, surrounded by the most awful death, amid the angriest and most fearful clamor, the day of Christ can break in. So wait and hope. Draw strength from above before you try to penetrate the darkness yourself. Such waiting enables *God's* rays to penetrate the world, invisible and yet palpable, so that those we meet, even if they have never thought about it, can sense when God is coming to them. We must be people who wait and are strong in our waiting. Then those around us will feel God's day for them.

**Most people are blind** (2 Cor. 4:4). They live only one day at a time, taking for granted the way things are. Yet, the way they live brings them no happiness; they find themselves swamped in an endless variety of misfortunes which they are unable to overcome. This is why God sent the Savior into the world. And still today, without us knowing it, he is helping countless souls, so that they are able to say: "I don't know how it's happened to me, but in some way I've been led through the need I was in!"

Jesus said: "I am the light of the world. Whoever follows me will never walk in darkness, but will have

the light of life" (John 8:12). The light of the world!
Deep down in the everyday corners of life that light
shines. Even if people do not recognize it, Christ is
there. Jesus is the world's Savior. He leads us ultimately from darkness into the light of eternity.
Despite toil, imperfection, and sin, under which we
still have to suffer, there is light, a tremendous light,
powerful and mighty with God's glory, unwilling
that any should perish, willing rather that every lost
person finds joy.

**If Jesus had not entered** into our human condition, into our sinful world, if in his holiness he had
distanced himself from us, where would we be? Time
and again, God has entered world history with all
its sin. God has allowed the brutality of the ages, all
the pride and desolation of humankind, to be loaded
onto his shoulders. God made use of David, even
though he had fallen deeply into impurity. He used
Nebuchadnezzar, too, as well as the stiff-necked Israelites. He even worked through the Greeks and the
Romans. God has gone where every kind of sin has
been committed. Isn't this amazing?

The same is happening today. Some Christians find God's involvement with human sin quite troubling. If God were really just and holy, how could he ever dwell amid those who are so full of sin? Doesn't this make God responsible for the crimes of war, for all godlessness and deceit in human history? But God the Father has remained among us precisely because he loves humankind and wants to lead us all out of our misery. It is through his very presence despite our sin that we find the strength to grow into the light of truth. So, don't get discouraged.

Jesus came into the flesh. He experienced the most depraved aspects of our human existence (Heb. 2:14–18). He has even borne the most gruesome of "Christian" eras since his death. Think back to the days of the barbarian invasions, when wild tribes gave their allegiance to Christianity and marched through the land shedding blood. Consider the Crusades, when people thought it the noblest of deeds to slaughter the Turks. What savage years followed the Reformation, during the Thirty Years War, when Gustavus Adolfus supposed Jesus accompanied him to war. Jesus at war? Jesus killing people?

Oh, what has he *not* taken upon himself over the course of the centuries?

From time to time consider how many situations caused by *your* own folly Christ has entered just to hold onto you. If Christ had let you go your own way, you would not be where you are today. This should be your hope for every person you meet and know.

**Whether people realize it or not,** they are under the rulership of our God (Rom. 11:32). This is why you should fight, with every ounce of energy God gives you, that every person on earth might come into the hands of Jesus (Col. 1:28–29). If you or I have to give up hope for a single human being, or for any place on earth, then Jesus has not risen for us. Then there remains a burden of death, agony, and darkness, and Jesus is not the light of the world. Neither you nor I can ever give witness to the light if we have to give up hope for anyone. For then everything gets reduced to human terms and we will not be able to bear the misery of this world, let alone our own.

**When you look** at the current state of affairs, it appears as if everything Jesus taught is impossible.

Humanity is striving after completely different things from what God wants. Because so many do not understand God, they fabricate some other god or ruler for themselves. This, in turn, leads people to stray even further from God, and in their disobedience they become more and more unhappy. God leaves them in their unhappiness, but he does so in order to have compassion on them, so the hour may come when they recognize that only he can help them. For God withholds his help only as long as we think our happiness lies elsewhere.

Society deals with criminals by locking them up. But God never does that. In disobeying God it is we who end up creating our own prisons. God did not make the hells people live in – it is we humans who create our own hells. It is we who create tormenting circumstances through our self-will and stupidity. This will continue to happen as long as we are not enlightened by God, who alone can lead us to life.

But for that reason you must not give up hope. God is ready, always ready, to break up any hell if people want him to; but we have to want it.

**Our faith in Christ** includes a measure of faith in humankind – the belief that through God, Christ, and the Holy Spirit humankind will arrive at something worthwhile. Your faith must achieve something that human society has always striven for but cannot seem to obtain. You have to believe that humankind will be able to represent something of God's eternal kingdom on earth. The world will not perish in distress. No longer will it be a disgrace to be human – it will be an honor to be true men and women. A yearning for this lives within every human breast – a primeval longing that cannot be destroyed. Jesus came in order to satisfy this longing. One day God's kingdom will come on earth. As a Christian you must believe in the future of humankind.

**Jesus came into the *world*** – yes, into our wretchedness and filth – for God loves the whole world, including all that has become diabolical and godless. "The people who lived in darkness have seen a great light" (Matt. 4:16). It was to the desperate, the condemned, the murderous, and those who no longer had any consolation or hope that Jesus came. To them it was given to see the God who loves them. Base everything you say and do on this fact: light has come into the darkness, and can shine into every pit of despair. This light is love. The gospel is God's love in our darkness. With every word of the gospel, God lays claim to the darkness – to sin, death, and hell – through his love. He loves each person, no matter how lost, as his child. You and I and those around us may be sinners. Yet from the cross God says to all of us, "I lay claim to you, not to judge you or condemn you, but to help you" (John 12:47). This is the light of the gospel and the darkness cannot overcome it (John 1:5).

# Reflection and Discussion Questions

## Foreword and Introduction

1. Jonathan Wilson-Hartgrove challenges us to expand our vision of the gospel. Can you think of examples of how the gospel that gets preached today is "too small"?

2. What does Bonhoeffer's phrase "religionless Christianity" (page xiii) suggest to you? Is it a helpful phrase? How could it be misunderstood?

3. Charles Moore asks several incisive questions about the challenge of representing the gospel in today's world (page xxi). What other questions come to your mind?

## Keep the Kingdom in View

1. Blumhardt repeatedly refers to the "kingdom of God." What, in a few words, do you think the kingdom of God is?

2. Blumhardt believes there is a growing movement of the Spirit around the world (page 2). What do you think? Is that true today?

3. Do you agree or disagree with Blumhardt's assessment of the Christian West (page 4)?

4. Blumhardt asserts that the greatest obstacle to God's kingdom "is in us and our clever solutions" (page 8). Do you agree? What other obstacles are there?

5. Why does Blumhardt not think much of the kind of Christianity that focuses on preaching eternal salvation? What else might the "good news" be about?

## Avoid Being Religious

1. Why is Blumhardt so critical of "religion" and of being "religious"? What do these words conjure up in your mind?

2. Blumhardt writes, "It is harder to lead people out of the swamp of their Christianity than out of the barbarity of sin and unbelief" (page 17). What do you think he means by this? Have you ever experienced this?

3. At first glance, Blumhardt appears to discount theology and church tradition (page 20). What role, if any, should theology and tradition play in our efforts to represent the gospel?

4. Blumhardt warns against misusing the Bible in reaching out to others. Can you think of ways the Bible gets misused in efforts to reach people for Christ?

5. Why is Blumhardt critical of baptism? Are there other church practices that may be doing more harm than good? Which ones?

6. Is there anything in this chapter that you especially agree or disagree with?

*Reflection and Discussion Questions*

## See How Christ Is Already at Work

1. Have you ever experienced Christ at work in hidden ways? When?

2. Where do you see traces of God, or "points of light," at work in the world today?

3. What cultural practices or values are "paralyzing the people" today (page 44)?

4. What do you think Blumhardt means when he says people "don't need to become 'Christians' like us" (page 45)?

5. In what sense does there "remain a precious jewel in *every* person" (page 51)? How can this be if we are all sinners and fall short of God's glory (Rom. 3:23)? If indeed there is a jewel in every person, how might this affect the way you relate to non-Christians?

6. Is there anything from this chapter you found especially encouraging?

## Remain among the People

1. Why does Blumhardt stress the importance of having genuine relationships when trying to represent the gospel? What has your experience been?

2. What does Blumhardt mean when he says that "Christ must come up behind people" (page 56)? Is this always the case?

3. How is "studying people" contrary to the spirit of Christ (page 58)? What are some examples of this?

4. In Blumhardt's experience, those on the margin of society have a greater hunger for God. Have you found this to be true?

5. Blumhardt claims that people "are afraid of the kind of revolution Jesus brings" (page 64). What kind of revolution is Blumhardt referring to?

6. People everywhere cry out for justice. What kind of justice do you think Blumhardt has in mind in this chapter?

## Open Wide Your Heart

1. Throughout this book, Blumhardt repeatedly affirms that everyone belongs to God. Does this mean that everyone is or will be saved?

2. What kind of people or groups do you tend to recoil from or look down on (page 76)? Why?

3. How might Christians relate to others differently if they avoided dividing the world into "us" and "them" (page 77)?

4. Blumhardt refers to an encounter he had with a kleptomaniac (page 81). Can you think of anyone in your life whom you should treat similarly?

5. Do you agree that Christ is sometimes more at work among non-Christians than Christians?

6. Blumhardt thinks that people's "thirst for God" is often misguided. Have you ever experienced this? How might

various "human thirsts" (page 86) afford an opportunity to bring Christ to people?

## Make God's Love Known

1. In what ways do people put limits on God's love?

2. Blumhardt reminds us to "love each person with Christ's love" (page 91). How is Christ's love different from human love?

3. Many people, including Christians, get bound up by anger under the guise of some righteous cause (page 93). Can you think of some examples? Why is this?

4. Blumhardt urges us to "endure whatever the world throws at you" (page 95). Does this mean we must be passive?

5. Are there any ways in which you struggle with being "bitter and cynical"?

## Show the Gospel

1. Truth is important, as Blumhardt reminds us, but what else is needed before unbelievers will respond to the gospel?

2. Blumhardt states that "religious clichés" get us nowhere (page 103). What kind of phrases do you think he is referring to?

3. From your experience, how does "pushing people into a religious experience lead to great disappointments" (page 105)?

4. What do you think Blumhardt means when he says, "To give thanks is to give witness" (page 106)?

5. In what way does Blumhardt suggest we be involved in politics? Are there any other ways you can think of?

6. Blumhardt writes, "Never before has the gospel been preached so far and so wide and yet with so little impact" (page 112). This was written over one hundred years ago. Do you think he would write the same thing today?

## Allow the Spirit to Work

1. From your experience, what does it actually mean to "let the Spirit do the work"?

2. Why does Blumhardt stress the importance of silence and of not using too many religious words (page 117)?

3. Are there any ways in which you are tempted to be "a knight in shining armor" (page 119)?

4. In Blumhardt's view, we should not tell anyone to their face about their sins (page 119). What do you think about this?

## Always Hope

1. Think of all the reasons you can why we must never give up on anyone. If we always remembered this, what effect would it have?

2. Have you ever met anyone who finds God's involvement with sin troubling (page 126)? If so, how did you respond?

3. Why does God leave people alone in their unhappiness (page 127)?

## Reflection and Discussion Questions

4. Take a look at the chapter titles again. Which one jumps out at you? Why?

5. Now that you've read this book, is there any thought or idea that stands out most?

# Sources

Blumhardt, Christoph Friedrich. *Christus in der Welt: Briefe an Richard Wilhelm*. Zürich: Zwingli Verlag, 1958.

———— *Christoph Blumhardt: Eine Auswahl aus seinen Predigten, Andachten und Schriften*. Edited by R. Lejeune. 4 vols. Zürich: Rotapfel Verlag, 1925–32.

———— *Hausandachten für alle Tage des Jahres*. Berlin: Furche Verlag, 1926.

———— *Vom Reich Gottes*. Edited by Eugen Jäckh. Berlin: Furche Verlag, 1925.

———— *Von der Nachfolge Jesu Christi*. Edited by Eugen Jäckh. Berlin: Furche Verlag, 1923.

# Other Titles from Plough

**Discipleship** Living for Christ in the Daily Grind
J. Heinrich Arnold
Thoughts on following Christ in the nitty-gritty of daily
life. Includes sections on subjects such as the inner life,
trust, forgiveness, community, leadership, suffering, and
the kingdom of God.

**The Awakening** One Man's Battle with Darkness
Friedrich Zuendel
Taken from the biography of Johann Christoph Blumhardt, here's a rare glimpse into how the eternal fight
between the forces of good and evil plays itself out in the
lives of ordinary men and women.

**Action in Waiting**
Christoph Friedrich Blumhardt
Pulsating talks and sermons on the kingdom of God and
the Sermon on the Mount. Blumhardt's active expectation
of God's kingdom shows us that our hope is not relegated
to some afterlife. Today, in our world, it can come, if only
we are ready.

**Evening Prayers** for Every Day of the Year
Christoph Friedrich Blumhardt
One of the few daily devotionals especially intended for
use in the evening. These prayers bespeak certainty in
God's nearness.

**Plough Publishing House** · www.plough.com
· 1-800-521-8011 · 845-572-3455 · PO Box 398 · Walden, NY 12586, USA
· Brightling Rd · Robertsbridge · East Sussex TN32 5DR, UK
· 4188 Gwydir Highway · Elsmore, NSW 2360, Australia